The Handbook
of Model-making
for Set Designers

This book is dedicated to all the students who have attended my classes at Northbrook College, Worthing; Mountview Theatre School, London; The University of Middlesex, London; The School of the Science of Acting, London; The Rose Bruford College, Sidcup; The Department of Drama at the University of Alberta, Edmonton, Canada.

The Handbook of Model-making for Set Designers

Colin Winslow

THE CROWOOD PRESS

First published in 2008 by
The Crowood Press Ltd
Ramsbury, Marlborough
Wiltshire SN8 2HR

www.crowood.com

British Library Cataloguing-in-Publication Data
A catalogue record for this book is available from the British Library.

ISBN 978 1 84797 019 0

ACKNOWLEDGEMENTS
So many people have offered such unstinting help and encouragement with this volume that I would be unable to rest comfortably without expressing my genuine gratitude to some of them at least, particularly the following: Lee Livingstone, friend and colleague, for patiently reading and correcting drafts, and her always shrewd advice; Guido Tondino and Victoria Zimski for their constant encouragement, support and friendship; Jan Selman, Chair of the Department of Drama at the University of Alberta for employment, support and friendship; Chris Want, Denise Thornton and Mel Geary for their friendly and enthusiastic help with digital technologies; Robert Shannon for sharing his office and bringing Captain Siborne's amazing model to my attention; Craig Le Blanc for supplying the photograph of the laser cutter at the Faculty of Environmental Design at the University of Calgary; Andrew Stocker, Customer Liaison Manager at Bristol Old Vic, for the photograph of the model of stage machinery in that theatre's foyer; Mark Johnson of the Edmonton Model Railway Association for the photograph of their impressive layout; Karon Butler of Dolls House Miniatures of Bath for the pictures of the Bath Circus dolls house; Josiah Hiemstra, for patiently taking many special photographs for this book, and losing his camera in the process; Robin Ramsdale, friend and reluctant hand-model. Finally, very special thanks to all my students, in Britain and in Canada, who have taught me so much, and to whom this book is dedicated.

PHOTO CREDITS
Holly Beck, Bath; Ellis Bros., Edmonton, Canada; J. Van Ens, The Edmonton Model Railway Association, Alberta, Canada; Barry Hamilton, Mold, North Wales; Josiah Hiemstra, Edmonton, Canada; Craig Le Blanc, Faculty of Environmental Design, University of Calgary, Canada; Peter Ruthven Hall, The Society of British Theatre Designers; Hojin Kim, Edmonton, Canada; The Sandra Guberman Library, Department of Drama, University of Alberta, Canada; Andrew Stocker, Customer Liaison Manager, Bristol Old Vic. All other photographs and illustrations are by the author or in his collection. All set and costume designs are by the author, unless otherwise stated.

Typeset by Simon Loxley
Printed and bound in Singapore by Craft Print International

CONTENTS

1   Introduction 7

2   Various Types of Set Model 17

3   Tools and Materials 29

4   Basic Techniques 49

5   Architectural Techniques 75

6   Painting and Texturing 91

7   Furniture and Dressings 103

8   Flown Scenery and Moving Parts 113

9   People, Trees and Other Organic Elements 121

10   Digital Techniques 129

11   Displaying and Presenting the Model 147

12   Constructing a Set Model Step by Step 155

Bibliography 173

Index 174

1 INTRODUCTION

'When we mean to build,
We first survey the plot, then draw the model;
And when we see the figure of the house,
Then we must rate the cost of the erection;
Which if we find outweighs ability,
What do we then but draw anew the model ...'

Lord Bardolph in *Henry IV, Part 2* (1597) Act 1, scene 3, by William Shakespeare

There is magic in a scale model, and the more detailed, the more accurate, the more true-to-life the model, the greater the magic it contains. We recognize this magic as children when we play with our dolls' houses or toy trains. A child's world has strict limitations, and it is hard to appreciate the concept of 'house' or 'train' when one's world is too small to encompass the object as a whole. However, through a model, children can explore the world about them without the intimidation of being considerably smaller in size than the adults the world is designed for.

For those of us who became fascinated by the theatre at an early age, a toy stage will always hold a very special magic: it allows us to experiment with exciting but impractical theatrical notions that we know could never become reality in a full scale production, but when combined with the creative imagination of a child, those miniature shows hold an enchantment of a kind rarely found

OPPOSITE: *A stylish dolls' house designed by Holly Beck, based on one of the famous Circus houses in Bath. Available from* Dolls House Miniatures of Bath. PHOTO: HOLLY BECK

RIGHT: *The elegant entrance hall of the Bath Circus dolls' house.* PHOTO: HOLLY BECK

in the real world. Limitations of mere size are far easier to cope with than the restrictions imposed upon us by considerations of budgets, safety, time, and the multitude of technicalities we have to take into account as set designers, and we can also ignore those stylistic restrictions we must impose upon ourselves in our grown-up, real-life design work. In our toy theatres, our imagination is given free range.

Ancient civilizations appreciated the magic contained in miniatures, as the beautiful models excavated from tombs clearly demonstrate. Egyptian tombs held scale-model boats, chariots and miniature rooms, elaborately furnished for use in the after-life, and the tombs of Chinese potentates

have contained whole armies in miniature. The fact that these objects are far too small to be of any practical use to their owners is ignored, and the scaled-down objects are seen as an adequate substitute for reality.

The scale models we build as set designers are, of course, quite different in purpose, but also contain a certain element of magic, for they constitute a prediction of the future, demonstrating a wish or desire for some future creation. Sometimes the creation turns out to be glorious, and sometimes (less often, we hope) it is doomed to failure. However, like all theatrical productions, once the creative act is complete, it has served its purpose and becomes redundant: hence the sad, dusty and battered models sometimes found quietly mouldering on the topmost shelves in theatre workshops, but still containing, under the dust, the shadowy record of a creative act.

In fact, the theatre is in itself a model of a kind, for the performances that take place upon its stage are not reality, but, however far removed, constitute a representation of some aspects of life itself: it is a model for Life. Many believe there are yet deeper layers in the model, that the world we inhabit is merely a model of some divine or cosmic after-life; or even, as Douglas Adams demonstrated in *The Hitchhiker's Guide to the Galaxy*, merely a huge model built by mice to work out the answer to the Meaning of Life, the Universe and Everything.

Occasionally, scale models attain a remarkable degree of notoriety: whenever an architect's model for a new building is exhibited there is frequently a cry of public outrage against the proposed design. In the crypt of St Paul's Cathedral we can still see the 'Great Model' that Wren had constructed to

Details of the impressive model railway layout of the Edmonton Model Railway Association in Alberta, Canada. PHOTO: J. VAN ENS

The Neptune, *a hand-painted Victorian toy theatre from Benjamin Pollock, still holds a special charm, in spite of its disregard for technicalities such as scale and sightlines that concern the set designer today.*

Sir Christopher Wren's 'Great Model' for St Paul's Cathedral was built from oak in 1673–74, at a scale of 1:24. It is 6m (about 20ft) long, high enough for a man to stand up inside, and cost as much as an average London house of its day. It was constructed with superb joinery and exquisitely worked cherubs' heads, flowers and festoons. Originally some of the detail was gilded, *and the parapets were surmounted with tiny statues, which were probably Wren's first commission to Grinling Gibbons, the master craftsman who produced much of the fine carving to be seen in the building today.*

PHOTO BY KIND PERMISSION OF THE DEAN AND CHAPTER, ST PAUL'S CATHEDRAL

demonstrate his concept for the new cathedral – but Sir Christopher Wren's beautiful model was considered deeply shocking at the time, and he had to resort to a degree of subterfuge to persuade the Church hierarchy of his day to accept his controversial design; and in the National Army Museum in Chelsea, visitors today can still admire a vast model of the Battle of Waterloo covering over 37sq m (about 400sq ft) and including 75,000 finely modelled and painted tin soldiers – but at the time it so offended the Duke of Wellington, because it demonstrated that he had not, in fact, won the battle single-handedly as he had claimed, that it

had to be severely altered to appease the irate Duke. Its builder, Captain William Siborne (1797–1849), having devoted years of work to researching and constructing the model, eventually died an impoverished and broken man. A model, it seems, can also contain the power to corrupt.

A set model, however, does not usually corrupt anyone, although it may occasionally shock, for despite its inherent charm, it is a model with a practical purpose. It is not a toy, and unless it eventually ends up in some kind of retrospective exhibition, it will be seen by only a very small group of people. In fact it has several purposes, in that a large part of a designer's work consists in communicating creative concepts to the team of people working on the show in production. The director, actors, stage management, set builders, property departments, costume and lighting designers need to be familiarized with the set designer's intentions long before they become concrete reality, and sheets of technical drawings, which need some skill to interpret, can never hold all the information the designer has to communicate to all these various departments, however detailed they may be.

This is where the scale model becomes preeminent. A glance at the model will show precisely what the designer has in mind, including many important aspects that cannot be indicated in the drawings, such as colour and texture. Anyone looking at the model will appreciate those aspects that affect his or her particular interest: the actor will note any steps or levels that he will have to negotiate in performance; the builder will notice any parts that might be tricky to construct or support; the costume designer will register the colours that the costumes will need to interact with on stage; and the lighting designer will note implied light sources and those places that might be difficult to light. Some directors like to use the model to plan their entire production in advance; others prefer to work more spontaneously, but will nonetheless use the model to keep a clear image of the set in their mind during the rehearsal process. The scale model is therefore an invaluable tool for all these people, and is generally considered indispensable to any production.

The lines quoted at the head of this chapter seem to indicate that Shakespeare appreciated the value of a model, although Lord Bardolph is not talking about the type of model discussed here – and in fact Shakespeare had no need of set models, because the Elizabethan playhouses provided him with an acting space which, through the power of language and his audiences' imagination, was perfectly adequate for any production in the players' repertoire. The more elegant and sophisticated performances at Court or in the banqueting halls of ducal palaces, however, presented some problems. Here, performances were required to

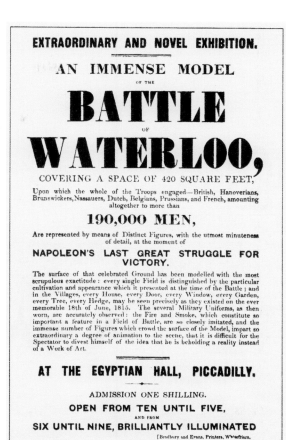

Captain Siborne's huge model of the Battle of Waterloo created a sensation when exhibited at the Egyptian Hall in 1838, but the Duke of Wellington objected to the inclusion of a large number of Prussian soldiers because it gave the (quite correct) impression that he had received a great deal of assistance from that quarter. Pressure was brought to bear upon the unfortunate Captain Siborne, and he was obliged to remove thousands of exquisitely detailed, 1cm (about 1/2in) high Prussian soldiers to preserve the Iron Duke's reputation of being solely responsible for the great victory.

Design by the architect and scene designer John Webb (1611–72) for Sir William Davenant's opera The Siege of Rhodes *in 1661.*
PHOTO: THE SANDRA FAYE GUBERMAN LIBRARY

take place in rooms with distinguishing architectural features such as fireplaces, doors and windows, and containing an assortment of domestic furnishings, and it would have been difficult for an audience to visualize, say, a wood near Athens or a stormy sea while looking at oak-panelled walls hung with family portraits.

The solution was to command the Court architects and painters to design spaces especially for performance. Many of the royal palaces of Europe contained extremely spectacular theatres, and travellers described the elaborate scenic effects they had seen on their journeys. Elizabeth I had been comparatively economical in her entertainments at court, but her successor James I – or more particularly, his queen, Anne of Denmark – was prepared to expend huge amounts of money on ever more spectacular productions. The celeb-

rated English architect and designer Inigo Jones (1573–1652) found that one of his principal functions at court was to design stages, machinery, scenery and costumes for elaborate masques of a kind that were never encountered in the popular theatres on the south bank of the Thames, nor even in the private theatres of Blackfriars or Whitefriars.

Inigo Jones greatly admired the skilful use of perspective that he had seen in Italy, and he introduced many of these effects into his work at the court of King James with spectacular success. However, the court painters used the tools and

Design for a painted cut-out piece from a prison scene by de Loutherbourg.
PHOTO: THE SANDRA FAYE GUBERMAN LIBRARY

techniques with which they were already familiar to produce their scenes; and their scenery, painted on large canvas-covered wooden frames that were bigger versions of the kind they used for portraiture, was seen literally as a mere background to the action, and there was little or no interaction between the performers and the scenery behind them. Even the machines designed to lower gods from painted clouds or to sink through the floor into a painted Hell, were decorated with flat profiled and painted scenic panels.

Usually, painters would produce a sketch of some kind before working on a scene at full size, and many designs still exist that have a super-imposed grid of pencil lines, clearly indicating that they were intended to be enlarged. It is a technique still used by scene painters today. It was a small step, therefore, to cut away the surrounding paper or card from the painted designs and assemble the several pieces to produce a simple model of the complete scene.

We know that as long ago as the early sixteenth century, the Italian painter and architect Sebastiano Serlio (1475–1554) was making models of the

13

Detail of the huge wooden model built by Edward Gordon Craig for Bach's **St. Matthew Passion.**
PHOTO: THE SANDRA FAYE GUBERMAN LIBRARY

fantastic machines he designed for the theatre – but his scenery still consisted basically of flat painted panels, supplemented by painted wing pieces. It was probably the innovative painter and stage designer Philip James de Loutherbourg (1740–1812), engaged by the actor/manager David Garrick (1717–79) to design scenery for the Theatre Royal, Drury Lane, who first used set models in the way we do today.

De Loutherbourg introduced a remarkable realism to the stage by the use of detailed cut-out set pieces such as rocks, mountains, houses, trees and fences; these often concealed rostra, steps or ramps behind them, so that actors could ascend the painted mountains and appear at the upper windows or on the balconies of the painted houses, thus interacting with the scenery instead of merely performing in front of it. He also introduced elaborate new lighting, with mechanically operated filters made from coloured silks to create special effects such as sunsets, moonlight, fires and volcanoes. Thus his sets were no longer solely dependent upon the skill of scene painters, and the combination of built pieces, transparencies and lighting tricks must have made the creation of scale models essential to convey the total effect of his innovative ideas. De Loutherbourg may be considered to be the first theatre designer in the modern sense.

As stage sets became more and more integrated into the action of the productions they contained, and three-dimensional built scenery replaced the flat, painted backcloths and wings, scale models came to be viewed as an essential tool in the production process throughout the twentieth century. The *trompe l'oeil* techniques of previous

14

ages were generally abandoned as plays were written that seemed to require a new kind of realism; box sets now suggested real rooms with real furniture, and three-dimensional architectural features such as built mouldings and panelling. Scale models were needed as an aid to designers and directors in establishing a precise arrangement of furniture and props appropriate to each production.

In the early years of the twentieth century, the more innovative designers and directors such as Adolph Appia (1862–1925), Edward Gordon Craig (1872–1966), and Vsevolod Emilievich Meyerhold (1874–1940) attempted to introduce a completely new type of theatrical performance that was more dependent upon the visual aspects than the textual, the actor becoming merely a moving part of the total stage picture. Their influence was far more extensive than the few productions they designed, and by the middle of the century, stage designers were expected to contribute to the conceptual aspects of a production to a much greater degree than ever before.

It was realized that stage scenery could go far beyond merely creating a theatrical version of reality, and designers began to employ an infinite range of conceptual ideas using many innovative techniques and new materials. It was no longer taken for granted that a stage set should resemble the physical location of the action as described in the text, and the scale model came to be seen as an essential tool to demonstrate the design concept. This meant that designers were expected either to develop model-making skills alongside their traditional rendering and drafting techniques, or to employ skilled model makers to do the work for them. Theatre design courses now usually include model-making in their syllabi, and students are expected to spend many hours honing their skills.

To many designers, the time spent building a model is the most pleasurable part of their work. It is a slow, usually solitary process that allows one to familiarize oneself with all the finer details of a design as it takes shape in miniature form; and simultaneously it offers a sometimes rare opportunity to listen to favourite music and reflect upon life in general. It is a time to aspire to sainthood.

2 VARIOUS TYPES OF SET MODEL

The set models with which we are most familiar are those beautifully constructed presentation models we sometimes see in exhibitions or as photographs in books on stage design. However, the designer will often make other models that may not look so impressive, and are usually seen by only one or two people closely involved with the production process – and sometimes only by the designer himself. The presentation model takes a very long time to construct so cannot be seen as an experimental tool, to be continually rebuilt and readjusted as an aid to the creation of a satisfactory design scheme. To avoid much wasted time and effort the design should be already established and approved before beginning the lengthy process of building the final model. Here we confront a typical 'chicken or egg' situation: how can the design be approved without the most effective method of demonstrating the designer's intentions? On the other hand, can we be expected to devote hours of work to a model that may need to be severely altered, or even abandoned altogether?

CONCEPTUAL MODELS

Sometimes a designer will build simple models as an aid to developing conceptual ideas. These models are very different from the finished presentation model, as they are rarely seen by anyone but the designer and the director, and little time is spent in their construction. They are usually temporary in nature, often involving little more than arranging a group of objects and some scrap card or paper that happens to be to hand at the time. They are often a type of three-dimensional collage.

The designer may find it useful to photograph a model of this type to keep a record of it for later reference along with the two-dimensional conceptual sketches. The addition of a cardboard figure will work a little magic and allow the viewer to visualize the assemblage of scraps at a human scale. Furthermore, this conceptual, putative type of model, however simple, can often be a great aid in formulating ideas. It serves the function of a

OPPOSITE:
The set for **What the Butler Saw** *being used in the paint shop as reference for the cloud-painted ceiling.*

RIGHT: *Experimental model built from 'found' objects.*

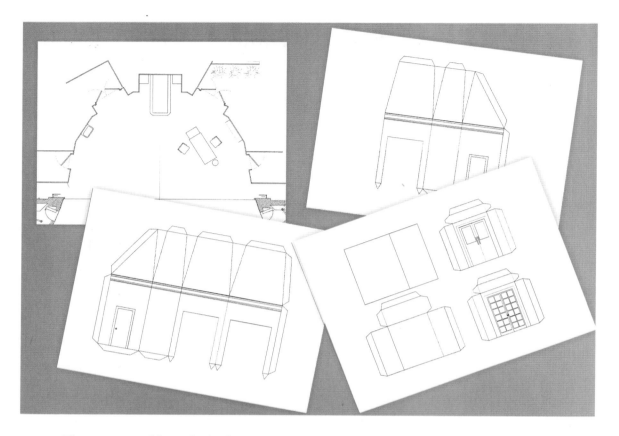

*ABOVE: **Elements copied from the working drawings, regrouped with added tabs to aid assembly, and printed on to thin card stock ready to be cut out for a speedily produced sketch model.***

*RIGHT: **Scoring card with the back of the blade for a neat fold.***

three-dimensional rough sketch, and its value should not be underestimated merely because of its unimpressive appearance.

SKETCH MODELS

The designer may produce several models before beginning work on the final version. These, however, will be 'working' models, quickly and easily constructed and intended to be broken apart or rebuilt in much the same way that we may erase or redraw the hasty conceptual scribbles in our sketchbooks. They are, in fact, three-dimensional rough sketches, and although often very crudely constructed, can form an invaluable tool in the design process.

Stage designers work to strict time scales, so it is not a good idea to spend a great deal of time making sketch models, whose function is merely temporary. The presentation model will inevitably

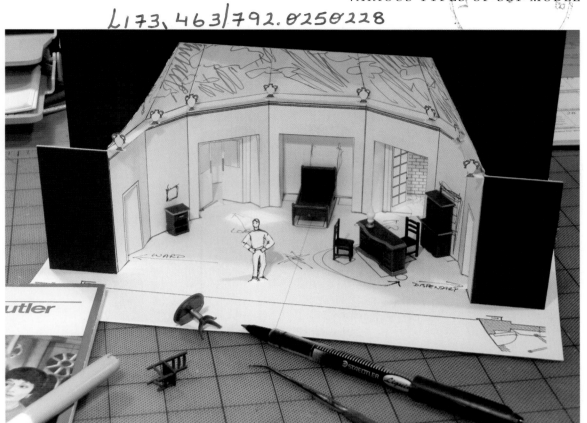

The sketch model for a production of Joe Orton's **What the Butler Saw** *photographed after a meeting with the director. Plastic furniture of an appropriate size bought from a toyshop has been used to plan furniture arrangements. The director was Ron Jenkins.*

take many hours to construct, so the designer needs to find a way to produce a sketch model within a matter of minutes. It is sometimes possible to sketch the main shapes on to scrap card, cut them out with a pair of scissors, and stick the pieces together with Sellotape to give a very quick impression of a set; but if you have already begun some working drawings, it does not take much time and effort to trace these off on to card, cut out the pieces and rapidly assemble them to give a reasonable impression of the finished set.

If you work digitally and are producing technical drawings by CAD, this process becomes even easier: use your CAD program to eliminate all the extraneous details in your working drawings such as borders and dimension lines, and add 'tabs' in appropriate places to help in gluing the pieces together; then print out the pieces on to thin card with a desktop printer, and you have a simplified

version of the set all ready to cut out and assemble like a model from a child's cut-out book. You will probably have to work at a comparatively small scale such as 1:50 (or ¼in to 1ft) to fit the pieces on to A4- (or 'letter'-) size sheets. Many corners that will have to be carefully cut and joined with glue in the final model can just be folded in the sketch model by 'scoring' the lines with a blunt blade and a metal ruler before folding to produce a clean fold.

It can be very useful to have a sketch model of this type available for creative discussions with

19

A white card model for Beth Henley's play **Crimes of the Heart** *ready for painting. The director was Kim McCaw.*

the director, because its rough, temporary nature means that one feels free to draw on it with felt-tip pens, cut pieces away with scissors or stick extra pieces on to it without destroying hours of painstaking work. A digital photograph of the model taken immediately following a creative meeting of this kind will serve as a reminder of the discussion, and can provide useful visual reference when revising drawings for the final model.

THE 'WHITE CARD' MODEL

Usually this is, quite simply, a presentation model at an intermediate stage of construction. Before a model is finalized with all its finished detailing,

texture and paint, it can be usefully viewed as a three-dimensional diagram of the set that can show many of the technical aspects involved in its construction even more clearly than the fully finished presentation model. For this reason, the designer may sometimes present his model in this form at an early production meeting. This is an additional reason to work cleanly, avoiding unsightly finger marks and smears of glue.

A white card model can be a very attractive object in its own right, such that sometimes the designer feels reluctant to soil its pristine clarity with a paintbrush. However, it will need to be painted eventually, so when assembling the parts of an unpainted model for presentation, take great care not to glue any parts together irretrievably that you will later need to separate for painting. It is better to provide a temporary fixing with drafting tape or pins here.

Photograph of unpainted model for
Charley's Aunt *at The Theatre Royal, York,*
digitally coloured and completed with an old
photograph of Oxford standing in temporarily
for a painted backcloth.

Presentation model for Opera Nuova's production of La Périchole. *Directed by Kim Mattice-Wanat.*
PHOTO: JOSIAH HIEMSTRA

A digital photograph of the white card model provides an excellent subject for experimenting with colour on your computer screen using software such as Photoshop, Corel Photo-Paint or Painter.

THE PRESENTATION MODEL

This is the most detailed and elaborate type of model. It is also the most interesting and attractive to look at, and certainly takes the longest time to produce. However, its purpose it not merely to delight its viewers, but to convey a large amount of detailed information. It can be seen as a three-dimensional coloured working drawing for the set, and this implies that it should be constructed as accurately as possible. It should be possible to take reasonably accurate measurements from it if necessary.

The presentation model should be well constructed so that it will not easily break apart when handled, and although it is not necessary to give the same amount of attention to the back and sides as the front of the model, they should at least be treated with neatness and care. A well made and finished presentation model demands a degree of respect and shows a professional approach on the part of the designer.

The amount of detail that should be included in the presentation model is open to debate: certainly, all parts of the set that need to be built in the theatre workshops should be represented on the model, including any built detailing. Furniture is also important, especially in a room setting, for the

22

Detail of set model for Opera Nuova's schools tour of **The Brothers Grimm.** *Directed by* **Kim Mattice-Wanat.**

model will not give a reasonable impression of the complete set without it. It will probably be thought necessary to include some dressings, too, especially the larger pieces, but a problem arises in deciding where to stop: a library set lined with bookcases, for instance, will not look very effective without the books filling the shelves. It will probably be desirable to show if the books are to be neatly arranged or just carelessly pushed in, and the books might need some indication of titles on their spines to make them look like real books – but the model maker might reasonably baulk at applying gold tooling and raised bindings to several hundred scale-model books. A fine artist does not necessarily improve a landscape by painting every single leaf on a tree, but uses his artistic judgment to convey his intention.

Architectural model makers often build presentation models for proposed buildings with a large degree of stylization. Sometimes they are purely diagrammatic models, with little or no attempt at reality. However, they normally work at a much smaller scale than is usual for stage models, and colours, if suggested at all, tend to be less significant and therefore much more generalized.

Some theatrical model makers, on the other

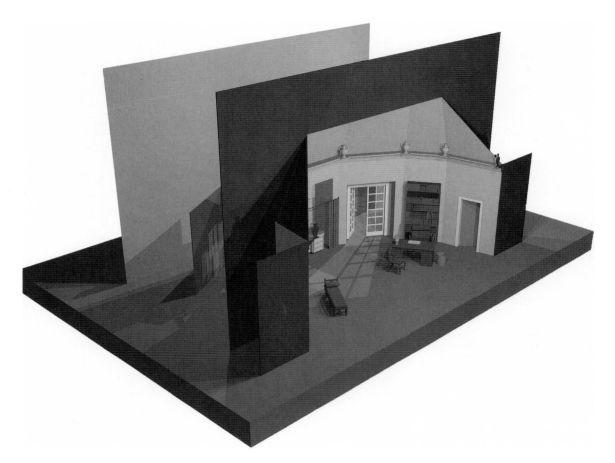

A digital model of the set for* What the Butler Saw *at the Timms Centre for the Arts, Edmonton, Canada. Directed by Ron Jenkins.

hand, delight in producing extremely detailed models, which can be quite wonderful to look at in all their exquisite detail. However, the sets that these models are intended to demonstrate can easily get lost in sheer admiration for the skill of the model maker. In the end, the amount of detail to be included is a matter for individual taste and judgment, and often becomes merely a question of the amount of time available for construction.

The same comments might apply to the figures included in some models: a scale figure is an extremely valuable adjunct to any scale model, allowing the viewer to gain an immediate sense of its scale. However, a whole cast of finely modelled and painted three-dimensional figures, delightful though they may be, can sometimes create the impression of an elaborate toy and confuse the more serious purpose of the model.

THE DIGITAL MODEL

Now that we all have computers in our studios, digital imagery in various forms is commonplace, and 3D modelling programs are becoming ever more sophisticated and user-friendly. Later in this book there is a chapter devoted entirely to digital techniques, but the computer model merits a mention here, for although it usually exists only in a computer's memory banks, it can still fulfill much the same function as a conventional model in conveying detailed information about the designer's intentions. Moreover, technological advances mean that it is now possible for a designer to produce a physical scale model from his computer, that can be handled and used in the same way as any other kind of model. The process is discussed in Chapter 10.

MODELS DESIGNED FOR EXHIBITION

You may wish to exhibit your work in an exhibition such as those organized by the Society of British Theatre Designers (SBTD), or the Prague Quadrennial Exhibition organized by the Organisation Internationale de Scéongrafes, Techniciens et Architectes de Théâtre (OISTAT). In this case the organizing body will define its specific requirements, but you should bear in mind that the model will need to be transported quite a long way to the exhibition space, and might be set up by someone else in your absence. Everything in the model should be very firmly secured in position to ensure that your model will be seen exactly as intended. You will be expected to pay an exhibition fee, and probably an additional fee to include a photograph of your design in the catalogue. Don't forget to arrange for collection or disposal of your model when the exhibition closes.

From time to time the designer/model maker is asked to produce a model specifically intended to impress potential backers or sponsors of an intended production. The management may be unable to proceed until a sufficient amount of money has been raised to cover costs, but backers (sometimes called 'angels' in theatre jargon) or other parties may be unwilling to invest until they are convinced that the production is already in preparation and will definitely take place. An impressive-looking model of the set design can help here, and you may be asked to produce one. However, bear in mind that this type of model does not have quite the same function as a normal set model, because in this case it is designed deliberately to impress, and will probably need a very high level of finish.

Pay some attention to the back and sides, and glue all pieces together very firmly on a strong base, because this model may be carried from place to place in the back of a car, and could come in for some rough treatment. Cover the bottom of the model with baize or felt: it may be presented to a group sitting around a highly polished boardroom table, and deep scratches on the surface of the table as it is passed around could jeopardize the whole production. The set shown in this type of model

---

Tactical Model-Making

It is not at all unusual for the designer's concept to surpass the budget allocated to a production, and the white card model is a good tool for estimating costs and trying to decide where cuts can be made to bring the set within budget. However, these discussions are frequently somewhat one-sided, for it is not usually taken into account that it is often just as easy (if not easier) to adjust the budget as the set.

It is not unheard of, therefore, for a designer to resort to subterfuge when these budgetary problems are anticipated: sometimes an element such as an elaborate backing, a large rostrum area, or some type of ceiling is very lightly glued into the white

card model, so that when the discussion reaches an *impasse*, the designer can make the handsome gesture of removing this element from the model, thereby giving the impression that he has made a considerable sacrifice in his design. This will usually encourage the management to make a reciprocal gesture, and a little more money is made available to make the remaining set viable, so all parties are satisfied.

This is, of course, basically dishonest, and the author cannot be expected to recommend it. He merely points out that it is a tactic that has been employed with remarkable success from time to time.

Part of the American pavilion at the Prague Quadrennial Exhibition of stage design in 2007.
PHOTO: PETER RUTHVEN HALL

may not, in fact, be the set that will eventually end up on stage – however, do not make the mistake of showing an over-elaborate set that might look far too expensive and impractical. Potential investors will want to ensure that their money is going to be well spent, and it is better to show a good, practical set and a model that, in this particular case, includes all the fine detail you can manage.

Don't forget, that although this type of model does not need to have all the practical aspects of the design fully worked out in detail, the higher degree of finish expected does require a lot of extra work on the part of the model maker. It should, therefore, attract a reasonable fee in addition to the normal design or model-making fee you may have been offered for the show.

From time to time the designer is asked if he would be willing to allow his set model to be exhibited in the foyer of the theatre. You may feel flattered when this happens, but ask some pertinent questions before you give your permission:

1. Where exactly will the model be exhibited? If it is just placed on an ordinary table it will be seen mainly from above, and may not look very impressive from this angle. A set model always looks its best when viewed at eye level.

2. Will it be possible to light the model effectively? A model does not always look impressive under normal lighting conditions, so a good light source, even if only from a carefully positioned desk lamp, can make a huge difference.

3. Will you be properly credited for your work? There should be a well placed label showing who designed the set and built the model.

4. Will the model be secure if left unattended? It is very difficult for anyone looking at a scale model to keep their fingers away, and after it has been poked and probed by a large number of fingers, the model will rapidly begin to deteriorate, and small loose pieces such as furniture will inevitably disappear altogether. A sign reading 'Please do not touch' is simply not sufficient protection.

5. Do you really want the audience entering the theatre for a performance to be able to anticipate that first exciting view of the set as the curtain rises, or in its carefully lit and presented pre-set state? By exhibiting the set model you could be guilty of spoiling a little piece of the theatrical magic that the director and designers have attempted to create.

3 TOOLS AND MATERIALS

SETTING UP A STUDIO

Not many designers are fortunate enough to enjoy the luxury of setting up exactly the kind of studio space they would really like to work in. The perfect studio would be spacious, with natural north light and adequate ventilation; an assortment of work surfaces, each designed for specific tasks; a sprung floor with easily cleaned vinyl covering; cork walls for use as pin-boards; a dedicated computer system; a spray cabinet; and adjustable artificial lighting. The list is endless. Unfortunately, most of us have to make do with working conditions that fall considerably short of the ideal, and those of us who have to work in a part of a shared office intended for a quite different purpose, or in one corner of a shared living space, would be grateful to work in even the most basic of studios.

'Studio' is a term that conjures up images of a spacious room with large skylights of the kind we have seen in films about the lives of great artists, or the first act of *La Bohème*. However, it really implies little more than a dedicated workspace, and every effort should be made to find a room – or at the very least, part of a room – that you can devote entirely to your work. Contrary to the generally held belief, the designer/model maker usually leads a solitary working life, spending long hours at a work table, drawing board or computer screen, and it is important, when the working day is over, to be able to leave your work as it stands and find it in exactly the same state when work is resumed the next day. It is not practical to clear the workspace at the end

Early stages in construction of the set model for **Street Scene.** *Parts for steps have been cut out and are being assembled using a plan of the unit as a guide.*

of each work session, so the kitchen table is out of the question.

The studio is required to be adaptable to a very wide variety of tasks. The model maker will probably also be a designer, so the workspace needs provision for drawing and painting in addition to surfaces for building and displaying models. The ideal studio will contain a sink with a water supply, and you will certainly need a large amount of shelving for storage and books. Remember that shelves intended for set models need to be considerably deeper than bookshelves. It is a good idea to store completed models on shelves built above head-height to keep them out of the way. And don't forget to provide somewhere reasonably comfortable to just sit and read.

Give careful attention to the type of chair or stool you will use. Remember the long hours you will spend sitting on it, and choose one that is ergonomically designed, with an adjustable seat and back to avoid possible back and neck problems. Take frequent little breaks for exercise, and if you find that aches and pains will not go away after a reasonable time away from your desk, you are probably using the wrong kind of seat or one that is not correctly adjusted, and should take steps to avoid long-term damage to your spine.

A sizeable pin-board area adjacent to the work surface is an item often overlooked. It is a good idea to cover a wall with cork or some other suitable surface that you can use for pinning up plans, pictures and drawings, or just those ephemeral odds and ends that can sometimes serve as a valuable source of inspiration.

Lighting
It is always more pleasant to work in a room lit by daylight rather than artificial light, but strong

sunlight streaming in through a window can sometimes constitute a serious nuisance, and often makes the screen of a computer monitor quite impossible to read. Artists throughout the ages have traditionally sought studios with north light, and this is indeed the ideal orientation for a studio window. However, few of us have the luxury of choice in the matter. Choose plain white or neutral-coloured roller blinds in preference to the slatted 'Venetian' type, as these will diffuse sunlight rather than merely breaking it up into streaks.

As theatre practitioners, our work will probably never be seen in daylight, but we also need to bear health issues in mind, and select artificial lighting that is tolerable for lengthy periods of close work, as well as a good light under which to assess colours that will eventually be seen on stage. Tracked lighting with an array of low-voltage halogen lights is very adaptable, and can form the basis of an efficient studio lighting system. It can be supplemented with additional light sources such as adjustable desk lamps where needed.

Electrical Outlets

Make sure there are sufficient electrical outlets for your needs. Nowadays we use a huge amount of equipment that needs to be plugged into a socket: your computer system alone will require at least six 'surge-protected' sockets, and you will need many other outlets for items such as desk lamps, music system, projector, battery re-chargers and coffee maker, to avoid the dangerous and inefficient use of multiple adapters. Make sure there are one or two sockets at a convenient height and in a handy position very close to your work surface for tools such as a soldering iron, a compressor for an airbrush, or an electric drill. These items are usually sold with a comparatively short cable to avoid the danger of tripping over one stretching across the room, so they need to be plugged in close to where they are to be used.

Storage Space

Some kind of storage space for tools is important, although this will vary in type depending on personal preferences and working style. Some model makers like to have their tools neatly arranged in labelled drawers according to type; others prefer to be able to grab tools from hooks or shelves located near to the worktable. A small set of storage drawers on wheels that can be pulled out to a handy position when needed is ideal.

Whatever method best suits your style and workspace, you need to make sure that your tools are readily and instantly available when you need them, and this implies a degree of organization. It can be extremely frustrating to have to stop work at some crucial point to hunt for a tool that has not been replaced in its usual position; you should be able to put your hand on any of your more frequently used tools without having to think where it is.

You will need a large waste bin close to your worktable. Model making produces a remarkable amount of waste material, and a bin that is too small and perpetually overflowing can be hazardous as well as messy. It is a good idea to buy a metal bin rather than one made of plastic, because almost all the materials disposed of will be flammable, and a fire in the waste bin is a serious possibility.

Models take up a great deal of space, and it will not be long before you will have accumulated enough to create a serious storage problem. The deep shelf above head-height described earlier is very useful, but will fill up alarmingly quickly, so you need to give some consideration as to what you will do with the models you have built. Perhaps the best solution is to take detailed photographs of each model for your portfolio, and then dispose of it.

Sometimes theatres like to keep models for their archives, but most, however carefully constructed, will deteriorate over time: they fade and warp, get crushed, acquire layers of dust, and eventually fall apart. It is sometimes possible to sell your models to interested parties, or just to give them away and enjoy the gratitude of a colleague. After all, once a production has opened, the model has fulfilled all those tasks expected of it, and becomes little more than a once glamorous, but now slightly embarrassing guest who will not leave after the party is over.

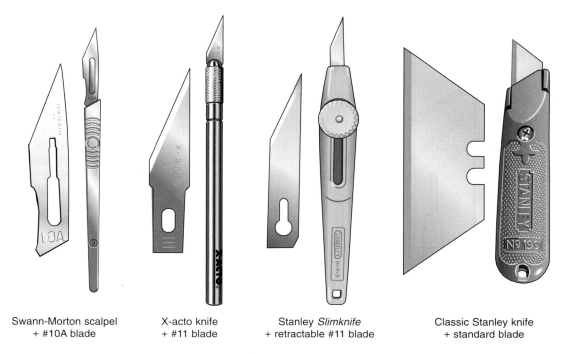

Swann-Morton scalpel
+ #10A blade

X-acto knife
+ #11 blade

Stanley *Slimknife*
+ retractable #11 blade

Classic Stanley knife
+ standard blade

A selection of cutting knives and blades.

TOOLS

It is quite impossible to offer a definitive list of all the tools needed for making models, as you will be working with a wide and eclectic range of materials, employing techniques that are often unconventional and will sometimes require unconventional tools. However, the first three items on the following list, namely cutting knife, metal ruler and cutting mat, should be considered essential.

Cutting Knives

The tool you will use most frequently is your cutting knife, so it is probably the tool you need to select with the most care. In fact you will probably end up with several, each one best suited for slightly different tasks.

The cutting knife needs to have an extremely sharp blade, so as soon as the edge begins to wear it should be replaced. This means that not only will you need a large supply of spare blades at hand, but also a knife designed to have its blade changed with as little trouble as possible. If you have to find

a screwdriver every time you change the blade, then you will tend to change it less frequently than you should, and your model making will suffer. It is also important that the blade fits very firmly into the handle without any movement when in use. Some knives are available with snap-off blades, making it very easy to obtain a fresh cutting edge, but the blade is never as sharp as one that has just been taken from its protective wrapping, and they have a tendency to wobble slightly in use. Do not sacrifice accuracy for convenience.

The blade you will need to use most frequently is one that tapers to a very sharp point. Manufacturers offer a very wide range of shapes and styles designed for a variety of purposes, most of which are quite useless for model making. You need the sharp point to be able to cut into corners and to cut cleanly around curves, so when you have discovered your preferred blade, buy them in boxes of, say, a hundred. It is much more economical to buy blades in this way than individually or in small packets of just three or five.

The drawing shows several different knives

31

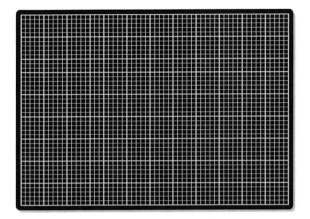

Cutting mat.

which will rapidly blunt the blade. Never cut against a scale rule: it will not produce an accurate cut, and its clean, sharp edge will very soon be ruined.

Cutting Mat

The third really essential item you need is a cutting mat. You cannot cut with a knife and straight edge without some kind of protection for the surface beneath. Never cut directly on to a tabletop or work surface; it is not the best surface to cut against, and will inevitably suffer irreparable damage. The vinyl 'self-healing' mats available from art and craft suppliers provide an ideal surface for cutting against. They come in a wide range of sizes, so choose the one that is most convenient for your particular working conditions. The cutting mat should be large enough for most cutting tasks (probably not smaller than A3), but not so big that it becomes an inconvenience when working in a limited space. The one illustrated here is 45 × 60cm (about 18 × 24in) and 3mm (1/8in) thick. The most popular colour is dark green, but several other colours are also available.

Choose a cutting mat with a work surface on both sides so that you can turn it over and double its life. It is a good idea to keep one side specifically for messy jobs that might damage the surface, such as carving or making steeply angled cuts; the other side will then remain in good condition for much longer.

If a vinyl cutting mat is not available, you will

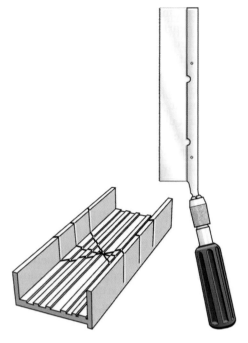

An X-Acto saw and mitre box.

need to find some other surface to cut against: it must be thick enough to protect the surface beneath it, but a piece of wood is not really satisfactory, as the cutting blade will have a tendency to follow the grain of the wood rather than the line you are cutting, and a sheet of metal will rapidly blunt the blade. Probably the best substitute for a proper cutting mat is a piece of thick strawboard such as that used for the back of an A3 sketchbook. It will deteriorate very rapidly, so do not cut on the back of one that is still in use. However, an old sketchbook can sometimes provide a very useful emergency mat.

Saw and Mitre Box

A model-maker's saw is essential when working in wood, and the saw and mitre box illustrated offers a good method of cutting wooden strips accurately to angles 90° or 45°. The saw blade fits into the handle of a normal craft knife. More elaborate versions are available that can be adjusted to cut to any angle, but they tend to produce less accurate cuts. Most of the saw cuts you will need will be at

Mitred corners in the moulding around a model door. The door is 3cm (about 1¹/₄in) wide.

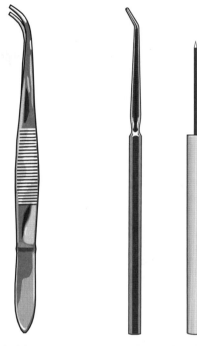

Angled forceps. *Biological probes.*

either 90° or 45°, and any other angles can be carefully marked out on the wood and sawn freehand. When using miniature wooden mouldings the saw and mitre box is invaluable for producing snugly joined corners with ease.

Other Useful Tools

Before you have made many models, you will discover a whole range of useful tools that suit your own particular work-style. Some model makers, for example, cannot work without a pair of tweezers or angled forceps at hand for manipulating very small parts, while others find a moistened finger-tip more versatile for picking up very tiny pieces.

Sometimes instruments not really intended for model making can be pressed into service. Inexpensive instrument kits intended for biology students often contain some very useful tools, such as the probes illustrated. They can be a great help when attempting to manipulate some tiny

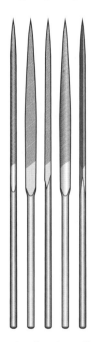

A selection of needle files.

Leather punch with revolving head.

35

Decorative paterae at the corners of a model door made with a leather punch and some painted detail. The circles are 5mm (³/₁₆in) in diameter.

piece of card into just the right position before the adhesive sets.

Needle files such as those illustrated are useful for a variety of purposes. They are available in many different shapes, and are best bought in a small pack of assorted styles. The points snap off very easily, so do not use them for jobs such as piercing holes into tough materials.

The leather punch is one of those tools not intended for model making, but very useful for cutting neat round holes into card. The revolving head of the punch illustrated on page 35 means that a range of different-sized holes can be made with the same tool, and the small circles of card punched out are also extremely useful for making small decorative features such as the *paterae* at the corners of classical door architraves, or threaded on to a round-headed pin to build up the 'neck' of a finial.

When using a leather punch to make holes in card or paper, always place a small piece of waste leather underneath the card, and punch through both layers. In this way you will make a much neater hole and prolong the life of the punch at the same time.

DRAFTING TOOLS

You will also need some basic drafting tools, but as a set designer making your own models, you will probably already have them for producing technical drawings. The drafting tools described below are the ones you will need for model making.

Pencils
The most basic piece of equipment for all design work: you will use pencils for transferring drawings to card before cutting out, and drawing structural elements that are not included on the working drawings, such as supporting structures beneath rostra and stringers for steps, as well as a thousand other small tasks. For most of these jobs

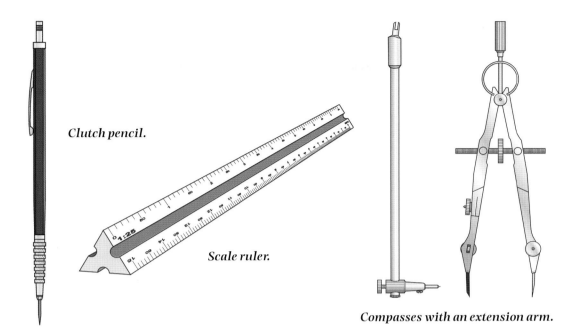

Clutch pencil.

Scale ruler.

Compasses with an extension arm.

you will need a fairly hard pencil such as a 2H, but soft pencils are also useful as a source of graphite to suggest metallic surfaces when painting models (*see* Chapter 6, page 99). Pencils are graded according to hardness: H indicates 'hard', and B indicates 'blackness' or the degree of softness. A clutch pencil is probably most convenient, as a broken lead is replaced with a simple click, so it is easy to maintain a sharp point. (Many designers do not realize that most clutch pencils designed for drafting contain a little lead pointer in the button on the top.)

Scale Ruler

An essential piece of equipment that is discussed in Chapter 4, Working to Scale (*see* page 55).

Set Squares

A pair of small set squares at 30°/60° and 45°/45° is particularly useful for rapidly checking right angles throughout the model-making process. Always check all right-angle cuts against a set square, and push a small set square into corners to check accuracy when gluing pieces together at a right angle.

Compasses

An obvious requirement for drawing circles, but a detachable extension arm is an essential addition for drawing the very large circles that are frequently needed for marking out revolving stages, or the edge of a curved forestage.

Circle Stencil

A very wide range of stencils is available for the draftsman, but perhaps most useful to the model

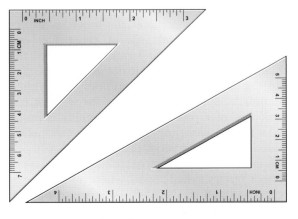

Small set squares.

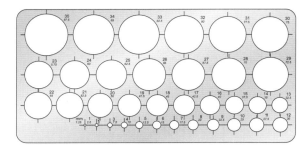

Circle stencil.

maker is a circle stencil, such as the one shown here. Very small circles can sometimes be tricky to draw accurately with compasses.

MATERIALS

The basic construction material used for set models is cardboard. However, this term covers a very wide range of products, and there is little standardization in the names of different types of card. There is no single type of card that is appropriate for all jobs, and you will probably need to use four or five different kinds in the construction of just one model.

Most types of cardboard are made from several layers of paper glued together to the thickness required, with white or tinted paper, sometimes with a specific smooth or textured surface, forming the outside layers. In cheap cards, these layers have an annoying tendency to separate quite easily, especially when cut into very small pieces for fine details, and sometimes the inner layers are made from a rougher type of paper that can make cutting difficult and can rapidly blunt the knife blade. Model makers do not generally need to buy the most expensive boards finished with a handmade paper surface intended for art work, but cardboard of a reasonably good quality is much easier to work with, and will produce better models than the very cheap varieties.

It is a good idea to keep a stock of different types of card, but try to find a space where the sheets can be stored flat. If they are left standing on one edge against a wall they can easily develop a curve that is sometimes difficult to eliminate.

Mount-board

(Alternatively known as mounting board, matt board, Bristol board.) Mount-board is used for most basic structures in a set model. It is a thick, sturdy cardboard, usually made with one side white and the other side coloured. Although the white side will be used most frequently for parts that are to be painted, a black side can be very handy for masking pieces, and a pale blue/grey board is useful for cycloramas. Mount-board is also available with both sides coloured if this is needed, and, at a little extra cost, it can often be bought with the same type of paper all the way through, so that cut edges are the same colour as the surface. It is available in several sizes, but most usually in sheets of 112×81.5cm (44×32in), and about 2mm ($^1/_{16}$in) thick.

Art Board

(Alternatively known as ticket card, museum board, and by various proprietary names.) Art board is a good quality white card available in a range of thicknesses usually designated by the number of layers used to make the card. Two-, three-, four- and five-sheet cards are usual. Check the surface: some makes have a slightly glossy, non-absorbent surface that makes it difficult to paint. It is easy to cut, leaving a clean edge, and the range of different thicknesses makes it particularly useful to the model maker.

Printer Card Stock

This is a good quality single-sheet card available in printer-size sheets (A4 in Europe, letter size in America). It is manufactured specifically for use with desktop printers, so is no thicker than will pass through the printer with safety. It has a good surface for painting, and it is often very useful to be able to print out small details from working drawings on your computer directly to the card.

Foam-Core Board

This is a specialist board made from a sheet of polystyrene foam covered on both sides with a layer of stout paper. It is available in large-size sheets in a wide range of thicknesses, from about 2 to 12mm ($^1/_{16}$ to $^1/_2$in). It is lightweight and very

This model, for Rookery Nook *at the Pitlochry Festival Theatre, contains several different kinds of paper used for floor coverings: the parquet floor is a printed dolls' house floor paper, darkened with diluted brown ink and varnished; the main carpet is flocked paper, sprayed with brown ink; and the small rug has been cut from a catalogue. The stair carpet and runner is made from painted blotting paper, folded over and pasted for additional thickness. The scale is 1:25.*

easy to cut, but the polystyrene will rapidly blunt the cutting blade, so it is a good idea to keep a heavy-duty knife specifically for cutting this type of board. Bear in mind that the foam-core can be severely attacked by most aerosol sprays, and some adhesives. Always test first if in doubt. White foam-core board often has a slightly glossy surface which can make it difficult to paint. However,

particularly useful to the theatrical model maker is the matt black board, with black foam at its centre, making it ideal for the construction of lightweight model boxes.

Papers

Cartridge (or poster) paper is a good paper for general use. A tough, fairly thick paper with a good surface for drawing and painting, it is inexpensive to buy and is generally available either in sketchbook form or in large, separate sheets. Rather like thin ticket card, it is particularly useful for making small sketch models.

Almost any kind of paper has its uses for the model maker: for example, the cheap absorbent tissue paper typically used to wrap bottles from a wine merchant is useful for pasting over rough carved or modelled objects to provide a good surface for painting. Several layers of absorbent paper and paste will set hard as *papier mâché*, and the object beneath can then be removed if desired.

'Flocked' paper, the decorative paper with a velvety pile often used to line gift boxes, is particularly useful for making model carpets. The range of colours available from suppliers is usually fairly limited, but plain white or grey paper can be coloured with inks or diluted watercolour as desired, and patterns drawn on with coloured felt-tip pens.

Blotting paper, still available although hardly anyone now writes with pen and ink, has a fibrous quality that thickens slightly and becomes very flexible when impregnated with paste, and will set hard when dry. It can be used to suggest upholstery fabrics when pasted over pieces of carved balsa wood for padded seats and chair backs on model furniture, or pasted and rolled to make miniature cushions or pillows. A strip of blotting paper pasted on to model stairs can be painted when dry to suggest a stair carpet.

Graphite Paper
Not a paper you will use as a construction material, but invaluable to the model maker for transferring designs from plans or working drawings to board preparatory to cutting out. It is merely a thin paper coated on one side with graphite powder, which performs the same function as old-fashioned carbon paper, but has the great advantage of *not* being indelible, so any surplus or temporary marks can be easily erased or painted over. Graphite paper can be bought from art stores by the sheet, or more economically, in small rolls. It is also available in several colours, including white, which is particularly useful for transferring designs to black card or board.

Wood
Next to cardboard, the material you will use most frequently in your models will almost certainly be wood of various types. Select the kind of wood that is most suitable for the task in hand.

There is a general impression that the best kind of wood for making models is balsa. However,

Woods for Model Making

Balsa wood (*Ochroma pyramidale*) grows in the rainforests of Central and South America, but the primary source of balsa for model making is Ecuador, where it is known as Boya, referring to its excellent flotation qualities. The name 'balsa' is from the Spanish word for a raft. It grows very quickly in small, scattered groups reaching a height of about 27m (90ft). Balsa wood is used in lifebelts, table-tennis bats and, most famously, was used by Thor Heyerdahl to construct his Kon-Tiki raft on which he crossed the Pacific in 1947.

Obeché wood (*Triplochiton scleroxylon*), also known as 'samba' or 'African maple', comes mainly from West Africa. The trees are very tall and slim, growing to a height of 45 to 55m (150 to 180ft). It is used in cabinetry (particularly for drawer slides) and for musical instruments and artificial limbs.

Basswood (*Tilia americana*), also known as 'linden', grows mainly in the eastern USA and Canada. The name comes from the inner bark or 'bast' used by native Americans to make rope and thread. A large tree, with a trunk diameter of about a metre (3ft), it reaches heights of 18 to 30m (60 to 100ft). It is used for furniture, musical instruments and Venetian blinds.

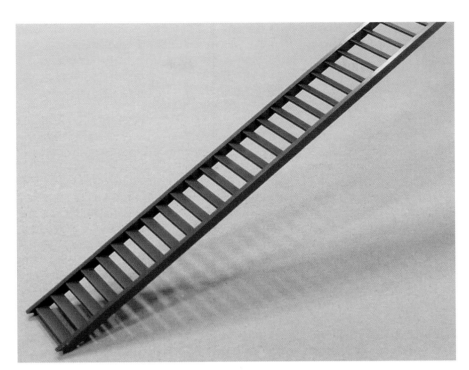

Scale open-tread steps by Plastruct.

Etched brass pieces by Scale Link. The bracket is about 1.5 × 1.75cm (about ¹/₂in × ³/₄in).

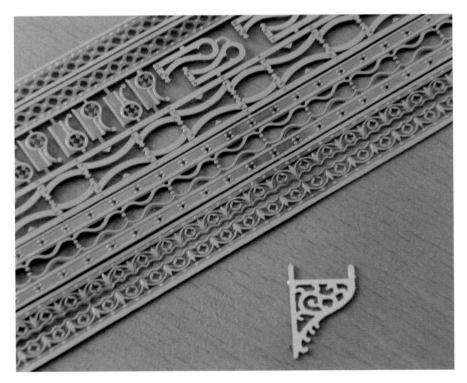

41

although balsa wood is very easy to cut and carve, it is far too brittle and coarse grained for many purposes, and usually the model maker will require a stronger wood with a much finer grain, such as obeché or basswood. These are both available from model-making suppliers pre-cut into the same kind of thin strips and narrow planks as the more familiar balsa wood. They cut or carve well, and will accept all the usual adhesives and paints.

Basswood is used to produce the miniature mouldings and turnings produced for use in dolls' houses. These are usually made in larger scales than those typically used for stage design, but the wide range of miniature balusters and moulding strips can often be trimmed down for use in set models.

Balsa wood is extremely easy to work with a craft knife, so it is very useful for making irregular or organic shapes such as rocks or tree trunks. It can also be used to carve the upholstered parts of model furniture. It is very absorbent, so it will need to be covered with soft paper and paste, or coated with a thin paste or artists' gesso to provide a good surface for painting.

When buying balsa wood, check the ends of the strips. You will sometimes see that they have been stained red or green to indicate the hardness of the wood: red is harder than green.

Many suppliers also carry stocks of other decorative woods such as mahogany, walnut or ash. These are usually sold in the form of thin sheets of veneer that are not suitable to use for construction, but can be cut into strips to make surfaces such as planked or parquet floors using the natural grain and colour of the wood. However, bear in mind that your builder will probably not be able to use these woods when building your set, so the wooden texture on the full-sized set will need to be reproduced using scene painters' techniques.

Plastic

Plastic is available for model making in several different forms. First, it can be bought in small sheets of various thicknesses, generally much smaller than sheets of mount-board or card, as they are intended for use in small-scale models. For this reason it is much more popular with architectural model makers who are working at very small scales, than it is with stage designers. For theatre work it is most useful for making very small details where cardboard has an annoying tendency to split apart into layers. The surface is not absorbent, so it will not receive water-based paints in the same way as cardboard, and will usually need some preparation, such as a coat of gesso, before painting.

Plastic rods of various forms are also available, such as round or square section, and 'I', 'T' or 'L' sections, which are particularly useful for making model girders when representing metal structures.

Probably most useful to the theatrical model maker are the component parts such as stairs (with 'open' or 'closed' treads), handrails and ladders made from white or grey styrene. The limited range of styles and sizes available means that they are not really suitable to be used for domestic or period stairs, but they are particularly useful for 'get off' or access steps, which are inevitably left until the last minute and can take much time and trouble to build from scratch. Some scale furniture at 1:25 or 1:50 is also available, but as it is intended for use in architectural interior design models, it is often somewhat stylized and consists mainly of office items such as desks and filing cabinets, rather than period styles.

Note that you will need to use a special adhesive for joining plastic pieces (*see* Gluing Techniques on page 64).

Metal

Most suppliers stock small sheets of different kinds of metal for model making, although these probably have only limited use for the set designer. Much more useful are the rods and tubes of various diameters. Copper and brass are perhaps most popular, as they solder easily, but aluminium is flexible, easy to cut, and can be used to suggest steel in a scale model.

Metal sheets etched with finely detailed parts such as ironwork brackets, railings, plants and metal furniture parts, ready to be cut apart, bent into shape and assembled, are available from good model shops. Etched metal parts are particularly

Glue

The first glues were the plant resins exuded by conifers. If you have ever tried to remove sap from your fingers after handling new timber, you will know that this has very good adhesive qualities. Six-thousand-year-old pots have been excavated, which show signs of having been repaired with plant resin.

However, most early glues were made by rendering animal products such as hooves, bones and hide, and it is this type of glue that has been used by carpenters from ancient Egypt to the present day. In its diluted form, known as 'size', it was used as a binder for the dry pigments used in scene painting until replaced by emulsion (or latex) paints in the 1960s.

In the early 1930s the first synthetic plastic material known as 'Bakelite' was developed, and it was immediately discovered that none of the glues in common use was effective with this new material. However, a German chemist named August Fischer developed a synthetic adhesive that was able to stick everything, including Bakelite. He named it after a Black Forest bird: Uhu.

Paste for gluing paper was made from rice flour by the Japanese hundreds of years ago, and it is still used in a more modern form for wallpapering. Paste was commercially available in convenient containers for use in schools and offices until the mid 1990s under the trade name of 'Gloy', but it has now generally been replaced by latex-based white glue.

'Superglues', containing cyanoacrylate, were developed as early as 1959, and form a very strong permanent bond. They were used to close wounds in place of stitches in the Vietnam war, and are still used for a variety of surgical purposes. Cyanoacrylate is an acrylic resin that sets almost instantly, triggered by hydroxyl ions in the trace amounts of water found on the surface of almost any object you may wish to bond. They are also found on objects you do *not* wish to bond, such as your fingers, so always use these glues with very great care.

suitable for making models containing delicate cast-ironwork such as Victorian conservatories. Many suppliers will take orders for custom etching, so you can now have your own designs cut into or embossed on to thin metal sheets – although this is not inexpensive, and is probably only viable if you need to have a large number of pieces cut. They can be produced from hand-drawn artwork, but work out much cheaper if you can produce your designs in a standard digital format such as *.dwg* or *.tif*, thereby avoiding expensive preparation time.

Model shops usually sell rigid or flexible wires in a range of gauges, some of them covered with a thin white plastic sleeve, but the old-fashioned cards of domestic fuse wire, in three or four gauges, are particularly useful for model making, though these are now becoming difficult to obtain.

You will need a pair of wire snippers or side cutters for cutting wire. Do not use scissors even for very thin wire, as it will very quickly damage the blades.

A pair of pliers is more or less essential when

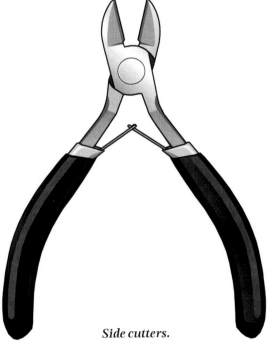

Side cutters.

43

Angled-nose pliers.

working with metal, and the angled-nose type illustrated here works best for most jobs. They are especially useful when soldering (*see* Soldering Techniques, Chapter 4, page 65).

Acetate

This is useful for making windows and other transparent parts of a model. It can be bought from art stores with a special coating to take inks or paints, or from stationery suppliers in sheets designed to fit a desktop printer. The printer sheets are usually coated on one side only, so check carefully that you are using the right side. Do not attempt to use the kind of acetate specifically intended for use in photocopiers, as normal inks and paints will always smudge on this type.

Acetate is particularly useful for stained-glass windows, but it can also be used creatively in other parts of a model: very fine details such as grilles or decorative ironwork can be drawn or printed on to it, and inserted into the model in such a way that the clear acetate becomes hardly noticeable.

Other Materials

Stage designers now work in such a very wide range of styles that almost anything can be pressed into use from time to time, so it is impossible to list all the materials a designer will use for making models. Set models have been made from practically every type of material, from concrete to macramé. The model maker will probably make a small collection of materials such as cork, decorative plastics, metallic papers and unusual fabrics that may one day turn out to be the perfect material for the job in hand. This collection of materials can also serve as a source of inspiration to the designer, in much the same way as a collection of pictorial reference material.

Real fabrics are hardly ever suitable to suggest fabrics in a scale model; even the finest fabric will not drape when cut into tiny pieces, as it will at full size. However, very fine cottons can be used for hingeing doors or covering model furniture, and a fine organza, especially in black, is particularly useful for making model stage gauzes.

Stage electricians use a foil-like, matt black, metallic sheeting known as 'black-wrap' manufactured for wrapping round stage lanterns to restrict the light beam or prevent light leaks. This can be extremely useful to the model maker, as it can be easily cut with scissors and bent into shape for making loose fabric covers such as tablecloths or bedspreads. It will retain its shape, and the matt finish means that it can be easily painted with gouache or acrylic.

Note: For paints, brushes and other useful tools for painting models, *see* Chapter 6, Painting and Texturing, page 91.

ADHESIVES

There is no single adhesive that is perfect for every job, and the kind of glue you use will depend upon the materials you are working with and the type of join you wish to make. Some glues dry too slowly and others dry too fast, and some are great for sticking card and paper, but will not hold metals or plastics. For successful model making, adhesives need to be selected with care. Whatever type of glue you use, remember that if you are going to paint the model with water-based paint, it should not be water-soluble when dry, or your model will probably fall apart.

PVA (Polyvinyl Acetate)

Produced by a number of manufacturers, and sometimes known as 'white glue', PVA will probably be the adhesive you use for most model-making

4   BASIC TECHNIQUES

Drawing

It is hardly possible to have any kind of discussion about design without sketching out a few ideas on a scrap of paper. These scribbles are not intended to be artistic masterpieces, but can be an invaluable way to communicate ideas in graphic form, and you should make a serious effort to acquire some basic drawing skills that you can use with ease and confidence. The designer/model maker will need three basic drawing styles, each of which has its uses:

1. *Technical drawing or drafting.* This is perhaps the most useful of the drawing techniques for the model maker, and it is the one that is easiest to acquire, for almost every line will be drawn with the aid of a drawing instrument of some kind. It is a purely mechanical form of drawing, which can occasionally be raised to the level of an art form by the really skilled practitioner. (Have a look at some of the amazing technical drawings by the celebrated Chinese/American designer Ming Cho Lee.)

2. *An ability to sketch ideas in a rapid, free style.* This is extremely useful when discussing ideas with a designer or director, as the simplest sketch can convey so much more information in a few strokes than a large number of words. This type of drawing depends to a large extent upon a degree of confidence and familiarity with the medium.

3. *The ability to produce really good drawings that display a high level of artistic ability.* This talent can be invaluable in almost any design field. However, few of us have a drawing skill of this kind, and it is, in fact, not essential in order to be a good model maker, or even a good designer.

Basic drawing skills can be acquired. Good technical drawing is a matter of learning the rules and becoming familiar with a range of drawing instruments. A good freehand style takes longer to acquire, but the secret is to draw continuously: carry a sketchbook and draw in it every day; get into the habit of drawing in spare moments, or when chatting with friends. To acquire a really good drawing skill, however, attend a regular drawing class, especially a Life Class, and you will find you will improve with surprising rapidity.

DESIGNING THE MODEL

Before beginning work on any model, devote a little time to deciding upon the best way to present the design you are working on in the format of a scale model. If you are building a model for a show with multiple scene changes that include moving trucks

The tavern truck for **The Bartered Bride** *is almost complete. The roof has been left separate until the rest of the model has been painted to facilitate access.*

and flown pieces, your model might encompass the whole stage area from wall to wall, including a method of hanging flown pieces in their correct positions so that the changes can be planned in advance using the model. However, a standing set frequently takes up only a part of the stage, and there is a distinct advantage in having a model that is a convenient size for storage and transportation. All masking should, of course, be included, so your completed model will probably extend well beyond the limits of the built scenery; but there is little point in building a huge model showing the entire

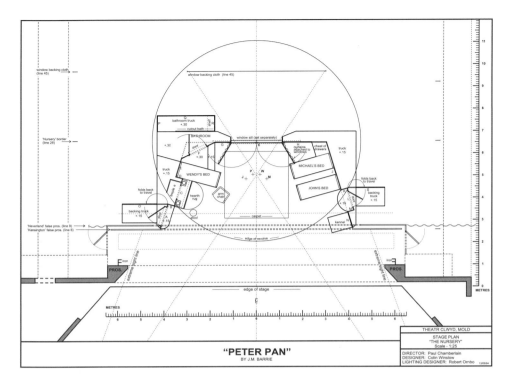

Stage plan for the first scene of Peter Pan *at Theatr Clwyd in North Wales.*

BELOW: *Drafting conventions used in technical drawings.*

stage to demonstrate a set that takes up just a small part of it.

The designer will almost certainly need to present the model several times at production meetings or the first rehearsal, so make sure that it is possible to reach all parts of it. Sometimes building the complete stage walls around a model can prevent easy access to the set itself.

Don't forget that flown pieces will need to be shown in their correct positions, so you may have to build a special structure to support these, even if they remain static throughout the show.

A really firm base for your model is a great help in maintaining solidity. MDF or blockboard at least 1cm (¹/₂in) thick makes a good base that will not warp. Plywood has a tendency to curl when painted, and this, of course, will have a disastrous effect on the model it may support. Glue all immovable parts firmly to the base for security.

A model of a set on a conventional stage should include the proscenium, although it is often useful to make this removable for better access to the set. If the set contains trap doors or access to levels

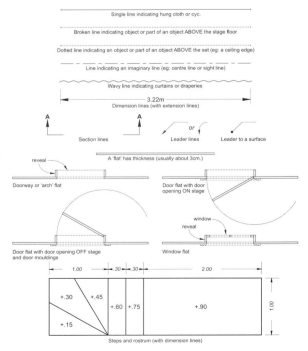

Working drawings for the first scene of Peter Pan *at Theatr Clwyd.*

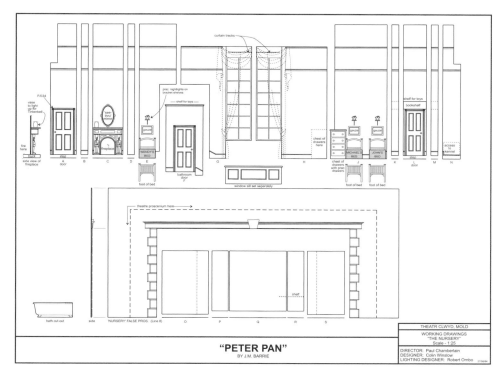

"PETER PAN"
BY J.M. BARRIE

| THEATR CLWYD, MOLD |
| WORKING DRAWINGS "THE NURSERY" Scale - 1:25 |
| DIRECTOR: Paul Chamberlain DESIGNER: Colin Winslow LIGHTING DESIGNER: Robert Ombo |

lower than the stage floor, you may have to build a base that is deep enough to contain them.

Finally, don't forget that you will need to paint the model after it has been built, so take care not to glue all the parts together in such a way that you cannot easily reach the areas you need to paint with a brush. The final assembly of all the parts takes place only after painting.

READING TECHNICAL DRAWINGS

If you are a designer/model maker, you will probably have produced some scale drawings before you begin to build the model, though they may not yet be finalized. If you are building a model for a designer other than yourself, you should be given some technical drawings to work from, so either way you need to become familiar with this type of drawing and to be able to read them with ease.

The Stage Plan
This is the most basic of the technical drawings the set designer will produce; however, remember that although this is an important drawing, it is very limited in the amount of information it can contain. It is rather like a map of a small town: it will show the streets and where some of the main buildings are situated, together with their relative sizes, but it will give you no idea of what the streets and buildings actually look like – another type of drawing is required for this. Similarly, the stage plan is not intended to show what a set will look like, only the precise positions of the scenery and furniture, and their relationship to the stage and auditorium. It is particularly useful for working out which parts of the acting area are visible to the audience, and which parts may be out of sight. The extreme sightlines or lines of vision, those from the worst seats in the house, are often indicated on stage plans with a broken line.

A stage plan cannot show the height of scenery: this is one of the functions of a sheet of working drawings; however, the heights of rostra, platforms or any other variations in floor level are usually shown with figures indicating heights relative to stage level. These figures are usually preceded by a

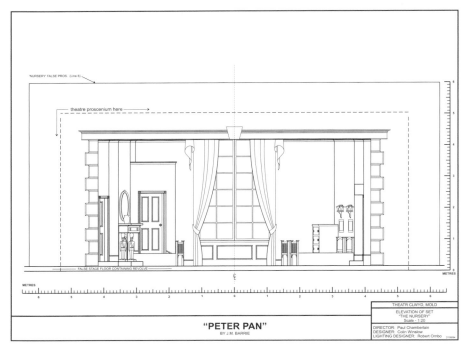

"PETER PAN"
BY J.M. BARRIE

THEATR CLWYD, MOLD
ELEVATION OF SET
"THE NURSERY"
Scale - 1:20
DIRECTOR: Paul Chamberlain
DESIGNER: Colin Winslow
LIGHTING DESIGNER: Robert Ornbo

Elevation of the first scene of **Peter Pan** *at Theatr Clwyd. (Note change of scale.)*

BELOW: *Stage section of the first scene of* **Peter Pan** *at Theatr Clwyd.*

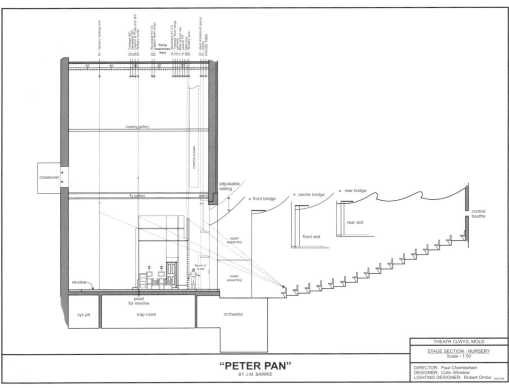

"PETER PAN"
BY J.M. BARRIE

THEATR CLWYD, MOLD
STAGE SECTION - NURSERY
Scale - 1:50
DIRECTOR: Paul Chamberlain
DESIGNER: Colin Winslow
LIGHTING DESIGNER: Robert Ornbo

Model of the Nursery Scene in **Peter Pan** *at Theatr Clwyd in North Wales, directed by Paul Chamberlain.* PHOTO: BARRY HAMILTON

'+' or '-' sign, or alternatively, set in a small circle. Remember that these numbers always show the height from the stage floor, not from each other; thus a flight of stairs might be labelled as +.15, +.30, +.45, +.60, +.90 (or +6in, +1ft, +1ft 6in, +2ft, +2ft 6in) and so on, on each step, suggesting that each individual riser is 15cm (6in) high.

WORKING DRAWINGS

Every piece of scenery to be built should be graphically described in the working drawings. They are the drawings that will be used in the workshops to build the set, and as they will probably be drawn at the same scale as the model, most parts of the set can be traced off directly from the working drawings. This has the added advantage that any errors in the drawings will probably be detected by the model maker long before construction is under way in the workshops. They form the basis for both full-size and scale-model constructions.

The front elevation is the drawing that gives the most immediate impression of the completed set. However, it should not be confused with a perspective rendering, for it is actually an isometric scale drawing showing each piece of scenery in its position relative to other visible parts. Any hidden parts are not usually indicated, and the

viewpoint assumes the viewer's eye level to be level at every part of the set – something quite impossible in reality.

Literally meaning a 'cutting through', the sectional drawing assumes that a cut has been taken right through the set, and a drawing made looking straight towards the cut side of one of the two parts. A centre-line section is most usual, but sometimes it is more helpful to make the imaginary cut through some other part of the set. The cutting line and direction of view is indicated by a section line terminating in directional arrows and letters for reference. (*See* Drafting Conventions used in Technical Drawings, page 50.)

Often several drawings will be required to describe part of a set or a special prop to be built in detail. Usually a plan, front and side elevations will be sufficient, but sometimes a rear elevation and section may also be needed. These are typically arranged on the page so that it is easy to relate them to each other, as shown in the drawing for Captain Hook's sleigh overleaf.

Before beginning any construction the model maker will need to transfer the designer's drawings on to card or mounting board for cutting out. Some

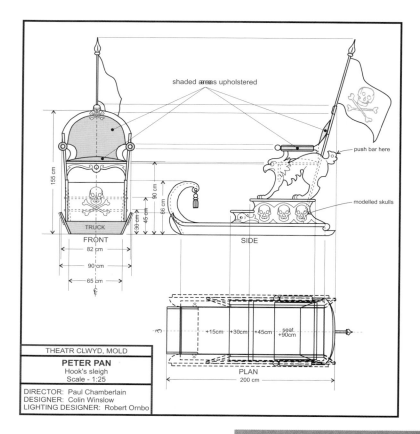

shaded areas upholstered

155 cm

90 cm

66 cm

45 cm

30 cm

TRUCK

FRONT

82 cm

90 cm

65 cm

push bar here

modelled skulls

SIDE

+15cm +30cm +45cm seat +90cm

PLAN

200 cm

THEATR CLWYD, MOLD

PETER PAN
Hook's sleigh
Scale - 1:25

DIRECTOR: Paul Chamberlain
DESIGNER: Colin Winslow
LIGHTING DESIGNER: Robert Ornbo

Prop drawing for Captain Hook's sleigh in Peter Pan *at Theatr Clwyd showing typical front, side and plan views.*

Model of Captain Hook's sleigh from the above sheet of drawings. The model is 8cm (3⅛in) long.

parts, especially interior supporting structures such as the 'stringers' for staircases, will need to be drawn from scratch with ruler, set square and pencil. Use a hard pencil such as a 2H for really fine lines. Scale rulers are really only intended for taking measurements, not for drawing lines. Of course, if you are using a scale ruler for marking out pieces, it is much more convenient to use the same edge for drawing, but try to force yourself to use a normal, flat ruler for drawing the lines, and you will obtain a higher degree of accuracy.

When working from the designer's technical drawings, you can trace off the parts to cardboard using graphite paper (see page 40). Attach the drawing to the card with drafting tape to make sure it will not shift while you are tracing, and slip the graphite paper between the sheet of drawings and the card. Trace the outlines of the shapes with a very sharp, hard pencil to produce thin, accurate lines, using drawing instruments as guides wherever possible.

Some model makers like to glue the working drawings directly on to the card with a spray adhesive, then cut out both paper and card. This technique can be very effective, but it does involve some dangers:

1. If the sheet of drawings is not glued very firmly to the card it will tend to lift and peel off when the model is being painted. On the other hand, if you use too much adhesive in an effort to play safe, you may find it bleeding through the paper and oozing from the cut edges, creating a sticky mess on the surface that is difficult to paint over.
2. Check that the paper used for the drawings is suitable for the paint treatment you intend to use. Sometimes photocopies are made on a slightly glossy, non-absorbent paper that is not easy to paint on. This is particularly important if some surfaces are paper and others are the 'naked' mount-board, because you may find that the paint dries to a quite different colour on each surface.
3. Some photocopy papers are quite heavy, so remember that this method will slightly increase the thickness of the pieces you are cutting out. This is not particularly significant on a single piece, but can sometimes make a sizeable difference overall when all the parts are assembled.

WORKING TO SCALE

All technical drawings are drawn to scale, and the scale used should be clearly specified on each sheet, usually in the title box. A scale is expressed correctly as a 'ratio', with two numbers separated by a colon, such as 1:25 or 'one to twenty-five'. This simply means that anything measured on the drawing must be multiplied by twenty-five to obtain the actual full-scale size. Most drawings for stage work are drawn at 1:25, but you may also encounter 1:50 or 1:20.

The USA is the only country in the world that still officially uses the old imperial system, so here you have to cope with 'feet' and 'inches'; for this reason you will find that the most frequently encountered scales in North America are 1:24 and 1:48. These scales are sometimes written as '1/2in to 1ft' or '1/4in to 1ft'. Do not be tempted to use the format '1/2in = 1ft', which is literal nonsense as obviously 1/2in is only 'equivalent' to 1ft, and can never be 'equal' to it.

The real advantage of expressing scale as a ratio is that it works for whatever system of measurement you may be using: thus you can measure in centimetres, inches, cubits, or even thumbnails, and simply multiply by the second digit to get the full-size dimension in the same unit of measurement.

Scale Rulers

Multiplying by twenty-five in your head is a tricky task for anyone not really proficient in mental arithmetic, but fortunately a very simple device is available that completely eliminates the need for mathematics: the scale ruler. This can look rather daunting at first, but it is really very easy to understand. Using this type of ruler you can read off dimensions as easily as if you are measuring the full-sized object.

The diagram shows typical markings along the

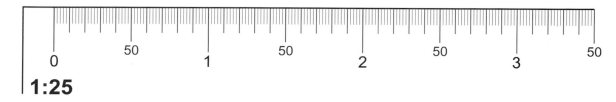

1:25

Reading a scale rule.

edge of a scale ruler. As most scale rulers carry several different scales along their edges, always check carefully that you are using the scale you need: this is indicated near the '0' end of the scale. The longest divisional marks indicate metres at this scale; the '50s' indicate half-metre divisions, and between these are 10cm divisions, and the smallest, 2cm divisions. Triangular-section rulers, such as the one illustrated on page 37, are particularly useful as they can carry more scales than a conventional flat ruler, and the sides are usually colour-coded to help avoid accidentally using the wrong side. You should become proficient at reading one of these rulers after just a few minutes' practice. When buying a scale ruler, make sure that the one you buy contains the range of scales you need. You can still buy scale rulers with the old imperial scales of 1:24 and 1:48 if you need them, but you may have to hunt for them in the UK and Europe.

Choosing an Appropriate Scale for the Model

The industry standard scale for set models is 1:25 (or ½in to 1ft in the USA). This scale produces models of a convenient size for most purposes, large enough to demonstrate to a group of people, but not so large that they become inconvenient to handle. Some model makers prefer to work at 1:50 (or ¼in to 1ft in the USA), but although these smaller models are convenient to transport, the very small scale means that much detail is lost, and presentation to more than one or two people is difficult. For these reasons, very small scales are usually reserved for preparatory or sketch models. The scale makes little difference to the length of time it takes to build a model.

The most convenient scale from a mathematical point of view is 1:20, because multiplying by twenty involves a very simple mental calculation that can be carried out in your head, whereas working at 1:25 means that a scale ruler is more or less essential if you are not a mathematical genius. However, models built at 1:20 become inconveniently large, and difficult to transport from place to place. You may sometimes need to work at a smaller scale than 1:25 when representing a very large stage to maintain a reasonably sized model, so calculate the size of the finished model before you begin, and adjust if necessary. (The writer has suffered the embarrassment of building a model that was too large to fit through the door of the train that was to transport it from London to Scotland.)

Some theatres have permanent model boxes of their stages specially designed to display set models, sometimes with built-in lighting and a method of supporting any flown pieces in their correct positions. These can save you a lot of work, but check the scale and what kind of base, if any, is needed for your model to fit the box.

It is obviously convenient to build the model at the same scale as the technical drawings, for many details can then be traced off directly. However, remember to check the scale on all sheets of drawings, because you may find (as with the *Peter Pan* drawings above) that the scale changes from sheet to sheet. The scale of a sheet of technical drawings can be changed if desired by a simple adjustment when it is photocopied, but remember that the scale in the title box will then be incorrect, so it is a good idea to write in the new scale immediately to avoid any confusion.

Changing the scale by redrawing by hand is a daunting task, but one that can be made much easier by the use of proportional dividers. This little known device is reasonably accurate and simple to use, and involves no mathematical calculations at all.

It consists of a pair of pivoted arms, rather like an ordinary pair of dividers, but with points at both ends of each arm, and a pivot point that can be moved up and down the arms by adjusting a screw. To use, you just move the pivot to the correct position on the scale etched along one of the arms, and measure elements on the drawing you wish to convert with the divider points. Then just flip the dividers over, and the points on the opposite side will describe the same dimension at the new scale.

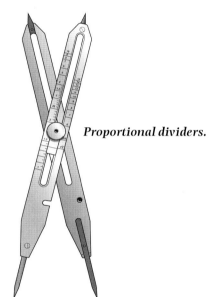

Proportional dividers.

Accuracy

A finished set model should be as accurate as possible. It should be viewed as a three-dimensional, textured and coloured working drawing. It is not intended to give merely a rough impression of what the full-sized set is to look like, but should be accurate enough to be measured with a scale ruler in the same way as a sheet of technical drawings. For this reason, a small scale ruler with no space between the end of the ruler and the zero mark can be a big help. It is sometimes possible to buy these from drafting suppliers, but you can easily make one for yourself by printing out the scale on to a sheet of card, or by simply cutting the end off a conventional scale ruler.

Using a home-made scale ruler to take measurements inside a model.

Cutting Card

An accurate scale model depends to a very large extent upon the model maker's ability to cut card with precision. All cuts should be made with a very sharp knife, and for straight lines, against a metal edge.

Here are some rules to bear in mind when cutting card:

Cutting mount-board with a scalpel and metal ruler.

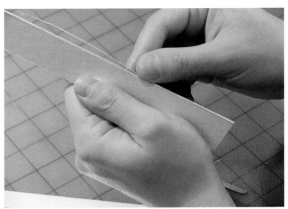

A piece of mount-board showing a neatly cut edge. *A piece of mount-board showing a badly cut edge.*

1. Always use a very sharp blade, and change the blade frequently. If you have used the blade for jobs such as carving polystyrene or sharpening pencils, change it before you start cutting out parts from cardboard. You may find it convenient to keep two knives, reserving one specifically for those jobs where you need a really sharp blade.

2. Always press very hard against the ruler to prevent any possibility of its slipping. In fact, you should press much harder against the ruler than against the knife. If your ruler slips while you are cutting, you will not produce a really clean edge.

3. Take particular care always to hold the blade at right angles to the card unless you are deliberately cutting a slanting edge. A slight change of angle between strokes will cause an inaccurate cut and a messy cut edge.

4. Do not try to cut right through the card in one stroke. If you are obeying rules 2 and 3, you can take as many strokes along the cut as necessary and still produce a neat edge. In fact, cutting in several shallow strokes will prevent tearing and produce a much cleaner edge than attempting to slice right through the card with a single swipe.

5. Never allow your fingers to extend beyond the cutting edge of the metal ruler. Your cutting knife is extremely sharp and can easily slip. Apart from the obvious fact that you will need all your fingers to complete the model, blood on cardboard can be very difficult to paint out, having an annoying tendency to bleed through successive layers of watercolour. Always play safe, especially when you are feeling tired after working for a prolonged period: this is the time when accidents are most likely to happen.

A well cut edge should be clean and sharp, and precisely at right angles to the surface of the card – in fact there is often a danger of cutting your fingers on the edge of a newly cut piece of card. Not only are these tiny cuts painful, they will also spread blood on to the card.

Cutting Corners

Most corners in your model will be made by merely butting the two edges together in the same manner as in the full sized set, the exposed edges concealed with paint. Check which way the pieces are joined on the plan, and do not forget to make allowance for the thickness of the cardboard where appropriate. Sometimes, however, you will want to mitre the corners for a neater join, particularly when building very detailed pieces such as furniture. Mounting board can be cut to an acute angle by merely holding the blade at an estimated 45° and locking the hand into position so that the

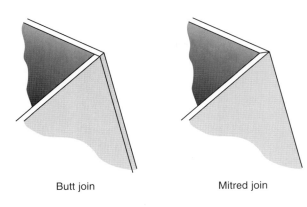

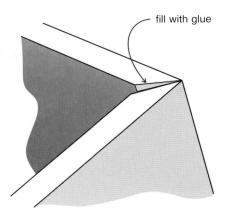

fill with glue

A butt join and a mitred join.

A mitred corner.

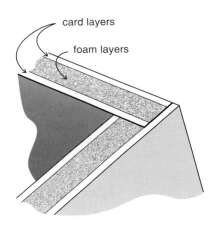

card layers

foam layers

Making neat corners with foam-core board.

angle does not change through the several strokes needed to slice through the card.

It is difficult to estimate exactly 45° when cutting card with a blade and ruler; however, if you always try to over-estimate slightly and cut angles that are slightly less than 45°, it is possible to join the two parts together at a right angle by checking the angle with a small set square and filling the slight gap in the joint with glue. This will not be seen, as the glue-filled gap will be at the back of the model, and will actually produce a stronger corner than the more usual butt join.

Corners mitred at angles other than 90° can be constructed in the same way, first cutting a small template to the correct angle from a piece of scrap board to hold in the corner to establish the correct angle when gluing the parts together.

Cutting Other Materials

Foam-core Board
This board is considerably thicker than mounting board, but is soft enough to cut right through with a single stroke. However, a single-stroke cut will not produce a really sharp edge, as some tearing will be inevitable.

Always use several strokes to cut through the board, and be sure to change the blade very frequently as the foam-core will blunt the blade more quickly than card or mount-board. The extra thickness means that a greater effort must be made

to keep the cutting blade upright to produce a good right-angled edge.

A major disadvantage of foam-core board is the unsightly cross-section revealed at cut edges. This can be particularly obtrusive when joining pieces together at a right angle. Where a really neat corner is required, the blade can be angled while cutting to make mitred joints, as with mount-board. However, it is often easier to cut through the top layer of card and the inside layer of foam only, leaving the card layer at the back. This thin flap of card can then be used to cover the cut end of the piece being joined to it, as shown in the diagram above, and trimmed to produce a reasonably clean, sharp corner.

Plastic Sheet

Plastic sheet requires a different cutting technique from cardboard: do not attempt to cut right through the sheet, but score it with a sharp blade, using a metal ruler as a guide as usual, but exerting a little more pressure than with card – because here you will make one cut only, cutting part-way through the plastic, then snapping the pieces apart along the cut you have made. For clean edges, break the scored sheet apart by placing it over a long hard object such as the handle of a craft knife, and snap by pressing down on both sides.

It is very difficult to cut curved or elaborately detailed parts from a plastic sheet using a craft knife. If you really need to do this, you should consider sending the job to a laser cutter, which will do it very quickly and with much greater accuracy than is possible by hand (*see* page 138).

Wood

Wood can be cut in the same way as mount-board, using several passes to cut right through it. There is often an urge to save time by applying extra pressure to the knife to cut right through the wood with a single stroke, especially when cutting very soft woods such as balsa. However, this will inevitably result in a rough, unsightly edge and should be avoided.

When cutting wood in the direction of the grain there is often a tendency for the blade to follow the grain of the wood instead of the line intended. Counteract this by exerting a constant pressure with the blade against the metal cutting edge. Cutting against the grain can be a little tricky, so you will need to use a large number of very shallow cuts along the same line to produce a really good edge.

Take special care to keep the knife blade at right angles to the cutting surface, especially when working with thick woods. The extra thickness will make any sloping edges particularly apparent, and it will be difficult to make accurate right-angled joints with them. Always use a model maker's saw and mitre box for cutting through wood strips.

Other Materials

Strips, rods, tubes and sticks of various materials are all used to create small details such as banisters, handrails, mouldings and furniture parts. They need to be cut with as much care as larger pieces, though they require slightly different cutting techniques.

Strips of mount-board frequently have to be cut to precise lengths for strengthening the back of a model, so use a metal cutting edge for accuracy even when cutting very thin strips. The square end of a metal ruler can be used to ensure a good 90° angle.

Wood and plastic strips, or rods, are best cut with

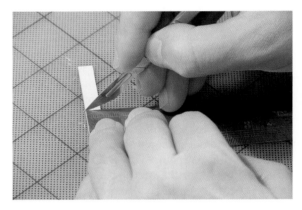

Using the end of a metal ruler to cut a card strip at a right angle.

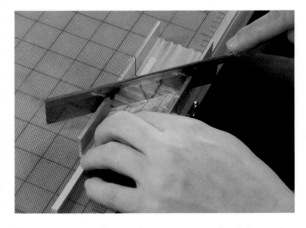

Using a saw and mitre box to cut an obeché wood strip at 45°.

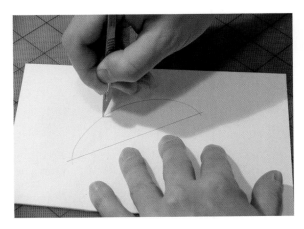

Cutting a freehand curve.

a small saw and mitre box as shown in the photograph, but very thin wooden dowel and turned pieces can sometimes be cut by rolling them on a cutting surface with the knife blade, then tidying up the cut with a flat needle file or fine sandpaper.

Cutting Circles and Curves

Cutting freehand curves from mount-board or card requires a little extra care. However, there are one or two points to be borne in mind that will make the job easier and more accurate:

1. Mark out the curve accurately with a thin fine line, either tracing from the working drawing with graphite paper and a hard pencil, or constructing a circle of the correct radius using a compass.
2. Cut from the inside of the circle, rotating the board as you cut so that you are always cutting the curve at a top right segment of the circle (*see* diagram); it is much easier to cut or draw this part of a circle accurately than it is the lower segments. Try it and you will see. (Reverse direction if you are left-handed.)
3. Use a very sharp blade with a fine point, and hold the blade upright so you are cutting with just the point only. Cutting with the whole length of the blade holding the knife at a shallow angle will create a tendency for the knife to move in a straight line.

4. Make the first cut very shallow, hardly cutting into the board at all, but taking great care to follow the line as accurately as possible. Continually turn the card as you cut, and use a little more pressure on each subsequent round, using the slight groove created on the previous round as a guide for the blade. After the first couple of rounds, more pressure may be applied to the blade as the cut should then be deep enough to keep it on the line. Always take great care to hold the knife at right angles to the surface.
5. Make sure you have cut completely through the card or board before attempting to separate the piece from the sheet: sometimes tiny sections of the curve will still not be cut right through, and these will tear if pulled apart, and make unsightly little glitches on the curved edge.

Note that when cutting out a part containing a curve or segment of a circle that joins directly on to a straight line, such as the curved top part of an

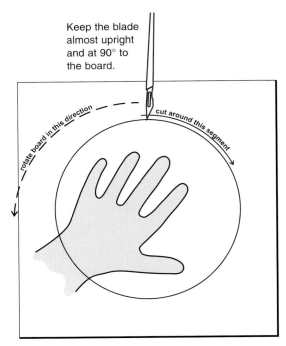

Keep the blade almost upright and at 90° to the board.

rotate board in this direction

cut around this segment

Rotating a circle while cutting.

The Latimer Circle Cutter

Required to cut a series of accurate circles from mount-board during a theatre design class at the University of Alberta, student Matt Latimer, showing little respect for his instructor's advice, shoved his craft knife through a strip of foam-core board, and using a pin as a pivot, began using this hastily improvised device as a circle cutter. The author (his instructor at the time) rashly remarked: 'If that works I'll go out and shoot myself.' It did, and I didn't. In fact it worked triumphantly well, and Matt subsequently delighted in demonstrating its ability to cut neat circles from such diverse materials as paper, card, polystyrene and chocolate cookies. For anyone interested in experimenting for themselves, Matt's circle cutter is shown in the accompanying photograph.

arch joining to upright sides, you will find you get best results by cutting the curved section of the line first, then cutting the straight lines to it using a metal straight-edge, and moving *away* from the previously cut curve. Working in this way avoids the little bump where the curve joins the straight line, which is inevitable if you cut the straight edges first.

Cutting Out Very Small Parts

Use a good quality card for very small details, and make sure your blade is extra sharp. Do not use over-thick card. For example, details that are to be cut from 1.25cm (1/2in) thick plywood in reality, require only a very thin card at a scale of 1:25 or 1:24, and this makes accurate cutting much easier. Remember that the tiny details on your model are just as important as the large pieces, possibly more so, as these are the pieces that will be examined most closely, and create the biggest impression on the viewer. No one will ever congratulate you on a faultlessly cut out circle, but a tiny, accurately cut fanlight will always draw some admiration.

Window panes create a special problem, involving cutting out a series of small, closely spaced rectangles, without cutting through the thin glazing bars between. The overall height of the French windows in the photograph is 18cm (7in), so the window bars are only about 3mm (1/8in) wide. When cutting parts like this it is important to get the point of the blade right into the corners. This is comparatively easy when cutting *away* from a corner, but difficult to do for the corner you are cutting *towards*, as the blade is pointing in the wrong direction. You can overcome this problem by systematic cutting: cut all the lines in one direction first, taking care to insert the point of the blade neatly into each corner, but stop cutting just before you reach the opposite corner. Then turn the card around and cut along the same lines, but inserting the blade into the opposite corner, and carefully joining up the cuts. When all the lines have been cut in one direction, turn the card through 90° and repeat the process with the lines running in the other direction. It is particularly important to keep the blade absolutely perpendicular to the surface of the card when using this technique.

Cut away all the internal areas before cutting around the entire piece, and do not remove the

This lamp bracket, measuring 3.5cm (or 1³/₈in) wide overall, was cut in one piece from card, with thin strips of card and small beads added to build up extra three-dimensional detail. It was soaked in cyanoacrylate to strengthen and harden it, then painted and varnished.

pieces of card you cut out until all the pieces in the part you are working on have been completely cut out. In this way, the cut-out pieces will continue to support the thin glazing bars while you complete the rest of the cuts. Finally, cut around the outside edges, and then enjoy the satisfaction of poking out all the tiny parts you have cut away from the centre of the piece, leaving a perfect window frame.

To be honest, you will be lucky if you manage to complete a large window such as the one shown above without cutting into *any* of the glazing bars, but one or two small slips of the blade can be neatly repaired with glue if necessary.

Small, fragile parts such as the lamp bracket above can be strengthened by carefully dribbling a thin superglue containing cyanoacrylate over it, allowing the glue to soak into the card. It is best to do this in two operations, holding the piece carefully at the top between tweezers and dribbling the glue over the opposite, lower half, then reversing the operation for the other half when the glue is thoroughly set. Take care not to glue the part to the tweezers by keeping the glue well away from the place where it is gripped. Cyanoacrylate

French windows from a set model.

has a disconcerting habit of spreading by capillary action to areas where it is not required, and sets very quickly. Treating with superglue in this way will make the part very strong – in fact you will probably break your blade if you try to cut it after treatment. However, it is dangerous: take very great care, work in a well ventilated area, wear a face mask, and always have some solvent handy. (*See* Safety Precautions on page 46.)

63

GLUING TECHNIQUES

Glue is messy. If it gets on to the surface of your model, it makes a white card model look dirty and unprofessional, and can sometimes be very difficult to paint over. If you get glue on your fingers when model making, stop and wash your hands immediately to avoid compounding the problem by spreading glue on to everything you touch.

The most common error when applying adhesive is simply using too much glue. More glue does not necessarily mean a stronger joint. Your aim should be to apply just enough adhesive in precisely the right place for the job in hand. Do not attempt to apply glue straight from a tube or plastic container, but squeeze a little out on to a suitable surface such as a piece of scrap card or a plastic lid, and apply with the point of a cocktail stick or a small strip of mount-board cut at a sharp angle. In this way you can apply a small amount of glue exactly where you intend with no danger of an overflow, and as the glue will already have begun to set a little before you use it, the setting time will be shortened and the parts being glued should quickly take hold, allowing you to carry on with other tasks while it sets fully.

You will need to work quite fast if using

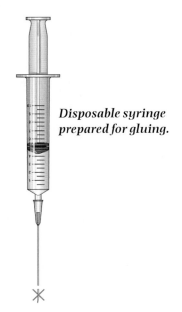

Disposable syringe prepared for gluing.

synthetic resin glues such as Uhu in this way, for this type of glue is usually designed to have a very short setting time. Squeeze out only a very small amount of glue at a time to avoid wastage.

Some model makers prefer to use a syringe to apply glue, and many model shops sell syringe dispensers specially designed for this purpose. However, it is a simple matter to make one for yourself from a cheap disposable hypodermic syringe available at any chemist's. The syringes and needles are sold separately. A 10ml syringe is the most convenient size for most jobs, with a needle of a fairly large diameter. It is a good idea to buy more needles than syringes, as you will inevitably need to replace them fairly frequently. Cut the point off the needle with a pair of side cutters as shown in the drawing, and dispose of it carefully. You will probably squeeze the sides of the needle together when you cut it, so gently hammer in a pin to open it up again, and keep the pin as a stopper to prevent the adhesive from hardening when the syringe is not in use.

You can fill the syringe with PVA glue or a synthetic resin glue such as Uhu. Push the needle firmly into place, then pull out the plastic plunger and pour or squeeze the glue into the syringe until it is about half full. Replace the plunger, turn the syringe point upwards and depress the plunger to expel the air bubble, like the mad scientists do in the movies. You can then place a tiny dab or a thin line of glue precisely where it is needed, without the danger of messy spills or sticky fingers. Don't forget to replace the pin stopper as quickly as possible after use: it doesn't take long for the glue remaining in the needle to begin to set, and then the needle is useless and will need to be replaced.

A syringe loaded with glue is particularly handy for emergency repairs after a model has been transported some distance for presentation, so include one in your portable tool kit – though this is probably not a good idea when travelling by air: even if you declare it openly at the baggage check, you will find it quite difficult to explain why you have a hypodermic syringe full of glue in your bag.

You may find that conventional adhesives do not work well with certain materials, such as plastics, acetate or metals. Specialized glues are available that are designed to cope with these materials, but when using any product for the first time you should always read the instructions very carefully, as some have to be used in a quite specific way. Do not ignore the recommended safety precautions; glues are notorious for giving off dangerous fumes.

For gluing plastics you will need to use plastic cement. These basically fall into two categories: some can be applied directly to the surface in the usual way, but be aware that many of them set extremely quickly and do not allow for repositioning. Plastic weld cement, however, works rather differently from other adhesives: the thin, clear liquid momentarily dissolves the surface of the plastic, welding it to the adjacent surface as it dries. To use this type of adhesive, hold the two parts together in position, and apply a little of the glue along the join with the small brush or applicator that usually comes with the bottle. The liquid will be drawn into the join by capillary action, and dries rapidly. It is not possible to use this type of glue in the conventional way.

Waiting for a slow-drying glue to take hold can be a frustratingly time-wasting experience, so many model makers like to use pins or drafting tape for a temporary hold while the glue sets. If you do this, be sure to use *drafting* tape as opposed to *masking* tape to avoid damaging the surface, and always remove the tape or pins when they have done their job. A model bristling with pin-heads looks unattractive and suggests a careless model maker.

Soldering Techniques

The model maker will inevitably need to work with metal from time to time, especially when the model contains parts such as metal grilles, handrails or metal-framed furniture. Soldering is not difficult, but you need to practise a little to acquire a good technique. Work through the following steps for any soldering job:

1. You will need a small stick soldering iron (*see* Soldering Equipment, page 46), a roll of 1mm-gauge solder and some acid flux.

A Word of Warning

Some glues, particularly synthetic resins, will dissolve polystyrene with remarkable effectiveness, so *do not use them* in any place where they might damage your model. This applies especially when using foam-core board. The glues are safe to use on the outside surfaces where the foam is protected by a layer of card, but can sometimes have a disastrous effect if applied to the polystyrene core. Check before use if in doubt.

Solder is the metal 'glue' that you will melt into the joint you are making, and the flux will help the solder to flow more freely through the joint and slightly etch the surfaces to be joined so that the solder can take a stronger grip. Some metals are easier to solder than others, depending upon the way they conduct heat. Brass and copper are probably the best, whereas galvanized metals are among the most difficult to solder efficiently.

2. Clear the workspace and protect the surface with a sheet of hardboard or plywood. Do not solder on your vinyl cutting mat, but a cork mat can form a useful surface, enabling pieces being worked on to be held in place with pins.

3. Cut all the metal parts to size with a metal saw or side cutters, and lightly rub with steel wool or sandpaper to slightly etch the surfaces to be joined and remove any oxidation or grease.

4. Assemble the parts to be joined and fix them temporarily into position. Do not rush this step: a little extra care taken at this stage will result in a stronger, more accurate join. You can use a copy of the working drawings as a template, but raise the metal parts from the paper surface by taping little pieces of wood underneath, or setting them into blobs of Plasticine. Keep the tape well away from the areas to be soldered. Carefully check that all

pieces are correctly aligned in both horizontal and vertical planes.

5. The soldering iron should be 'tinned': this simply means cleaning it and applying a very thin coat of solder to the tip. First clean the surface with sandpaper or steel wool, then heat the iron and wipe the tip quickly on a wet cloth. Melt just enough solder on it to cover the working tip. Quickly wipe again with the wet cloth. If the iron starts to look uneven or has black spots on it, it may need to be re-tinned.

6. Apply a small amount of flux to all joints with a pointed wooden stick (a cocktail stick is ideal). Note that soldering flux is corrosive and poisonous, so if you get any on your skin, wash immediately with plenty of soap and water, and do not breathe in the fumes of zinc chloride given off by the heated flux.

7. Using the tinned soldering iron, heat the metal just beside the joint until the heat is transmitted to the area to be joined. This may take about a minute, depending upon the type of metal you are soldering and the heat of the iron.

8. Touch the solder to the joint and remove the iron when the joint appears to be complete. Note that the solder is melted by contact with the heated joint only, *never* with the soldering iron. Attempting to melt the solder directly with the heated iron will inevitably result in a messy joint. Carefully wipe the joint with a damp cloth to cool the area. A good joint looks bright and shiny, whereas a bad joint will look dull.

9. When the joint is complete and thoroughly cooled, wash off the flux with warm soapy water and leave to dry. Omitting this step may result in the flux corroding the metal.

Note: Using solder can be hazardous, so check Safety Precautions on page 46.

STRENGTHENING TECHNIQUES

Cardboard is a remarkably strong material when used correctly, but it has a major inherent dis-advantage: it will always warp when drying out after it has been dampened. This is particularly inconvenient for the set modeller, because almost all the card we use in our models will need to be painted eventually, and usually with a water-based paint. Consequently we must take some serious steps to overcome this tendency to warp.

Cardboard warps because paper is made from organic matter that expands and contracts with humidity. As most cardboards are built up from several layers of paper, when the surface layer is painted with water-based colour it will inevitably expand, and the dry under-layers will attempt to restrict this. As the wet top layer dries again, it contracts, and pulls the under-layers in the opposite direction, thus producing a permanent curve in the board that will resist attempts to straighten it by placing it under weights. The solution is to make every effort to prevent the board from warping in the first place, by re-inforcing any large areas of cardboard at the back. Some model makers do this with strips of wood, but in fact it will be found that strips of mount-board glued on edge provide a much stronger support than thin strips of wood, which can be bent with comparative ease.

The larger the span of cardboard, the more strengthening it requires. Generally speaking, any area of card that is larger than about 5 to 8cm (2 to 3in) in any direction, and is intended to be painted or textured, will need to be supported. If in doubt, add extra supports: it can be extremely disheartening to see a beautifully finished white card model, to which you have devoted hours of work, gradually twist out of shape as it is being painted. Mark out a logical grid in pencil for the supporting structure on the back of the cardboard before you begin, and cut plenty of strips of mount-board to the thickness required. (Do not forget to allow for the additional thickness of the card itself if the overall thickness of the piece is crucial.) These supporting strips are best glued into position with a resin-based glue such as Uhu, as water-based PVA glues can sometimes soak into the card and cause it to warp in spite of the strengthening strips. If you have to use PVA glue, take great care not to use too much: there

Strips of mount-board glued on edge at the back of a model to add strength and prevent warping.

is a tendency to think that because you are applying glue to areas that will not be seen in the finished model, a lavish application straight from the container will save time and make it stronger. In fact, quite the reverse is the case.

CONSTRUCTION TECHNIQUES

Rostra and Platforms

Many models require rostra of one form or another. They may be quite small, intended just to support a few props or a piece of furniture, or they may form a very elaborate construction big enough to cover a large part of the acting area, containing steps or stairs and several intermediate levels. In any case, it is a good idea to start a model by building any rostra required, as they generally form a basis upon which other parts are to be built. For this reason, they need to be particularly solidly constructed.

Start by tracing off the rostrum tops from the stage plan on to mount-board. Sometimes the design will require a strip of 'nosing' to be fixed along some edges of the rostrum. The set builder will usually do this after the rostrum has been built, by attaching a rounded strip of timber

about 3 or 4cm (1 or 1½in) deep to the top edge, so that it gives the appearance of projecting a little beyond the side. It is particularly common in period interior settings. In the set model, however, it is usually more convenient to add nosing where it is needed when cutting out the rostrum top: cut the surface piece slightly larger on the sides where you need the nosing, and leave it slightly proud of the supporting side pieces. Nosing is frequently not indicated on stage plans, so check which edges (if any) need it, and add it before cutting out the rostrum top.

Once cut out, turn the mount-board over and mark out lines on the back for a gridwork of supports. It is not sufficient to support the rostrum top around the sides only, unless it is very small. Generally speaking, there should be no unsupported area larger than about 5 to 8cm (or 2 to 3in). Remember to set back the sides a little from any edges where you have added extra for nosing.

Cut strips of mount-board to act as supports for the rostrum, taking care to allow for the thickness of the board used for the top. Try to cut enough strips to complete the job: it is annoying to run out and have to stop to cut more just when the rostrum is almost complete. Start by gluing into position the

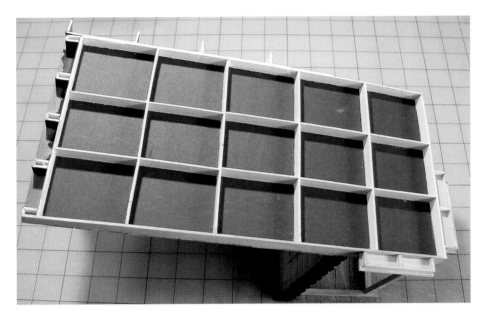

Grid of supporting strips of mount-board glued beneath a rostrum in a set model.

side of the rostrum most clearly seen by the audience. Use sufficient, but not too much, glue. If using PVA glue, remember that it is water-based, and if you use too much it will soak into the card and cause it to warp. Check with a small set square that the strips are glued at right angles to the rostrum top. When all the supporting gridwork is in place, turn the rostrum the right way up and place some books on top until the glue has set really thoroughly.

Dealing with Curves

Not all rostra consist solely of straight lines, and those with curved sides require special treatment: a piece of mount-board will not bend through more than one or two degrees before it begins to buckle, so you will need to take measures to counteract this tendency. The usual technique is to make a series of parallel shallow cuts along the *convex* side of any supporting strips of board that will need to be bent around a curved side. Try to keep the cuts evenly spaced, at right angles to the edge of the strip, and of a uniform depth without cutting all the way through the card.

The strip can then be bent easily into the curve desired. If the curve is a *concave* curve the scored side will not be seen inside the rostrum, but a

Preparing a strip of board to bend around the curved side of an irregular shaped rostrum.

convex curve will show the rather unsightly cuts on the outside of the model. These can be hidden by gluing a strip of paper over the offending side. Cut the paper strip slightly wider than needed so you can trim it neatly to the edge with a knife after it has been glued into position. Make sure the paper is very firmly glued to the model, or it will tend to peel off when painted. The rest of the rostrum should be supported by a gridwork of straight strips in the usual way.

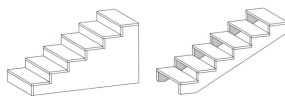

Model dais with curved risers covered with glued paper to hide cuts. Each step is 6mm (¼in) high.

Solid stairs and open-tread stairs.

Staircases and Steps

The set builder will usually build a staircase around *stringers*, timber formers fixed under the steps for support (*see* diagram below). You can build model steps in the same way, cutting stringers from mount-board and gluing the risers and treads on to them. The set builder will probably add any nosing required to the steps after they have been assembled, but when building a model, it is easier to incorporate nosing into the tread by simply cutting the tread a little wider so that it protrudes slightly beyond each riser.

When building solid steps, the stringers may be extended right to the base as shown in the diagram above, forming a solid side. One or two spacers cut from mount-board and glued between the two sides will give added strength.

When cutting stringers for model steps it is very easy to become confused when allowing for card thickness. To avoid this, it is worth taking a little time to draw a diagram like the one below. It is drawn to the scale of the model, but the treads and risers are drawn to the *actual* thickness of the card being used, indicating the way the treads and risers are to overlap each other, and the amount allowed on the front edge of each tread for nosing. Note that, in this arrangement, the riser on the bottom step is shorter than all the others. Stringers can be traced off from this diagram ensuring accurate dimensions when the model steps are assembled.

Open-tread steps are made in exactly the same way as solid steps, but omitting the risers. This type of steps is particularly suitable to represent 'get-offs' or access steps, although in practice the set builder will probably recycle stock steps for these jobs, as they will never be seen by the audience.

Curved or winding stairs can also be built using the 'stringer' technique if it is possible to run a pair of parallel stringers along the length of the stairs (*see* diagram at top of page 70). Draw the lines of the stringers on the plan, spacing them as wide

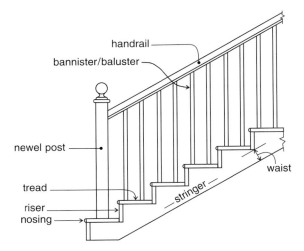

Parts of a staircase.

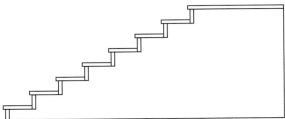

Section through model steps showing distribution of treads and risers.

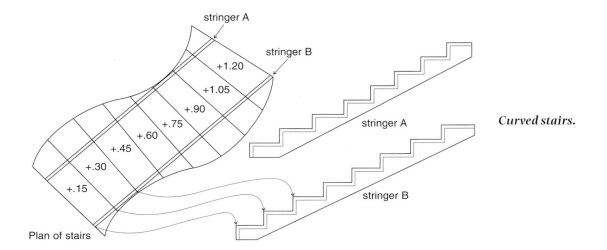

stringer A

stringer B

+1.20

+1.05

+.90

+.75

+.60

+.45

+.30

+.15

stringer A

stringer B

Plan of stairs

Curved stairs.

Completed curved stairs model.

Stair unit in set model. The upper steps are constructed on supporting stringers, the lower steps are built using the 'stacking' technique. Each step is 6mm (¹/₄in) high.

apart as the curve of the stairs will allow. It is now possible to draw the shape to be cut out for each of the stringers, bearing in mind that although each riser will be the same dimension, the width of each tread will vary depending on where the stringer intersects the tread on the plan; so measure the depth of each individual tread along the stringer drawn on the plan, and transfer it to your drawing of the stringer on the board.

When the stringers have been drawn out, you will need to remove an allowance for the thickness of the board you are using from each riser and tread (shown by the red lines in the diagram). Trace off the shapes of the treads from the plan, marking the position of the stringers on the back, and cut out all treads and the two stringers. Cut strips of board for the risers and assemble, gluing all the parts firmly into position.

An alternative method of constructing model steps is to treat each step as a separate rostrum, glue supporting strips beneath each one, and then glue them all together in a stack to form the complete run of steps. This technique is particularly suitable for constructing small corner units, or steps where it is not possible to run stringers through them. (*See* illustration above.)

Occasionally quite irregular steps of a more organic nature are required, and in this case the 'stacked' technique described above is the best way to work. Cut out each step level from the stage plan as a separate rostrum, and support in the usual way. Supporting strips fitting around a curved or an undulating edge will need to be scored as described above (*see* Dealing with Curves, page 68), and unless they are to be heavily textured after assembling, conceal the cuts with paper glued firmly around the side of each step.

The Model Box

This is not, strictly speaking, a box at all, but a stylized representation of the theatre proscenium, or any permanent structure surrounding the set, to place the set model into its context. The model box is inevitably left until last, so frequently has to

*Set model
showing method
of suspending
flown pieces.*

be speedily built to meet deadlines. However, try not to sacrifice solidity to speed. Do not waste time building a very detailed representation of the proscenium or auditorium, as during a performance they will almost certainly be unlit and all attention focused on the set itself. Try to create the same effect with your model. However, the model box does require a little careful planning.

Start with the base board: most parts of your finished model will be glued to the base, and it will need to be painted and textured in the same way as the stage floor in your set. Choose some really firm material such as blockboard or MDF. Mount-board, foam-core board or thin plywood will simply not be strong enough; it will inevitably warp when painted, and will possibly ruin the model. The base should be at least 1cm (about ½in) thick, preferably thicker. If you need to do any fine painting on the floor of the model, then bond a sheet of mount-board to it with a spray adhesive for a better surface.

The base should include most of the stage surrounding your set, but if you have a small standing set on a large stage with no elaborate scene changes, then you might prefer to limit the size of the model box to just beyond the part of the stage occupied by the set. This will result in a smaller model that is easier to transport and handle. If, on the other hand, you are designing a set with multiple scene changes, where scenery will need to move on and off the acting area and be stored in the wings, then it is best to build the whole of the stage from wall to wall so that the set model can be used to work out changes and available storage areas in advance.

Black foam-core board is the most popular material for building the proscenium and any stage or auditorium walls you decide to include, but for extra solidity you may prefer to build them out of plywood. Model boxes are usually painted black. This will not only suggest the effect of a lit set in a darkened theatre, but also has the advantage of clearly demonstrating which parts of your model show the set as designed, and which parts are intended to show existing structures around the performance space.

Your model box should include borders, legs and any other masking surrounding the set, even if this is just soft black masking to be pulled from stock. It is not necessary to suggest realistically hanging drapes for this; black corrugated card is excellent for suggesting black drapes in a semi-stylized way, but pieces of black mount-board cut to size will be perfectly adequate if this is not available. Don't forget to paint any cut edges that show, if they are not black already. Never attempt to use real fabrics for masking in your model, even though they may, in reality, be made from fabric; it never behaves in a model as fabric does at full size, and will inevitably look clumsy and inaccurate. Include the 'cyc' if one is planned, but although this, in reality, will probably be white, it is a good idea to make it a neutral grey in the model, as the cyc will only rarely be lit as pure white, and a stark white background can give a false impression of how the set will look on stage.

Whether you are using stock masking, or masking that has been designed specially for the show, some arrangement will be needed to support it in the correct positions. Fabric borders and legs will be hung from flying lines in reality, so it is a good idea to use a similar technique in the set model: build the side walls of the model to a convenient height so that any flown pieces can be suspended from rods or lengths of thin dowel spanning the whole box and supported by the walls at either side. Backcloths and any other flown set pieces can be treated in the same way. You can cut slots in the top of the side walls to hold them in the correct positions, the slots labelled with the numbers of the flying lines on the sides of the box. In this way, flown pieces can be easily removed or lowered into place to demonstrate scene changes in a multiple-set show.

Take care that your completed model box does not restrict access to the set model itself. If the walls are too high it will be difficult to reach inside to demonstrate features when the model is being presented. It is sometimes possible to cut away parts of the walls to provide access at each side, but a better solution is to make the entire model box separate from the base, so that it can simply be lifted off for demonstration purposes.

5 ARCHITECTURAL TECHNIQUES

Many set models involve architectural features of some kind, and much time will need to be devoted to building period doors, windows and fireplaces with details such as recessed panels, architraves and door frames with period mouldings. It is, of course, impossible to cover every eventuality, and the techniques described below should be viewed as examples that can be adapted to many other related situations.

DOORS

Doors are, perhaps, the architectural feature most frequently encountered, and should be built into the set model so that they operate efficiently,

OPPOSITE: *Cutting out wrought-iron railings from thin card for the façade of a New York brownstone for Opera Nuova's production of Kurt Weill's* Street Scene. *Directed by Brian Deedrick.*

opening in the same way as the door in the finished set on stage. First make the flat into which the door is to fit; the plan will probably indicate a *reveal* of some kind around the door opening. This is simply a 'thickness piece' designed to give the impression that the wall is actually considerably thicker than the 3cm (1¼in) that is the usual thickness of a stage flat. In practice, the builder will probably screw pieces of timber cut to the thickness required down each side and along the top of the door opening on the back of the flat, so that when the door is open, the audience will perceive this as the thickness of the wall. Note that reveals are added only where they can be seen by the audience: it is not usually necessary to build the entire flat to the full thickness.

Cut the door a tiny bit narrower all round than the doorway that is to contain it, remembering that there will be a slight build-up of paint when the model is finished, so allow for this to get a good

Three model doors in contrasting architectural styles. The first two are made from layered card as described below, and the door on the right is built from obeché wood. Each door is about 8cm (3¼in) high.

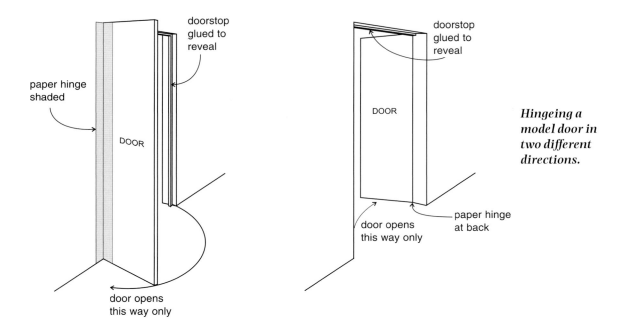

paper hinge
shaded

doorstop
glued to
reveal

DOOR

door opens
this way only

doorstop
glued to
reveal

DOOR

door opens
this way only

paper hinge
at back

*Hingeing a
model door in
two different
directions.*

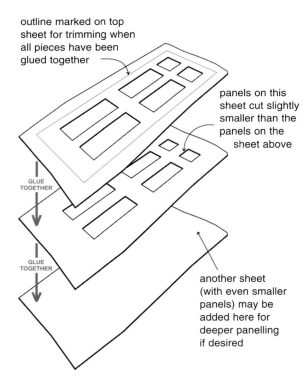

outline marked on top
sheet for trimming when
all pieces have been
glued together

panels on this
sheet cut slightly
smaller than the
panels on the
sheet above

GLUE
TOGETHER

GLUE
TOGETHER

another sheet
(with even smaller
panels) may be
added here for
deeper panelling
if desired

Making a model panelled door.

fit. A hinge can be created from a strip of paper glued to the side of the door, and to the side of the doorway or the back of the reveal, depending on which way the door is to open (*see* diagram above). Check the stage plan for the direction of opening. Fit a doorstop inside the reveal as soon as the door has been hinged into place; this will stop the door from being forced right through the reveal, tearing the paper hinge. The paper hinge can be concealed behind the door moulding added later. Some model makers prefer to use a thin fabric hinge for extra strength, but providing adequate doorstops are fitted, paper is quite strong enough, and is much easier to hide than the bulkier fabric.

Recessed Panels

Period doors typically contain a number of recessed panels, and these should be built into the doors in the set model. The set builder will construct these with wooden rails and stiles framing the panels, complete with slim strips of decorative moulding fixed around the inside of each panel. However, the model maker will need to use a rather different technique to produce the same effect.

Three model windows in contrasting architectural styles. The windows at each side are cut from card, and the centre window is built from obeché wood.

Trace the outline of the door and panels on to a sheet of thin card, then cut out the panels, but do not cut around the outside of the door until later. Place another sheet of thin card underneath, draw around the inside of each of the panels, and then mark out another rectangle a small distance (say, 1.5mm or 1/16in) inside each panel. Cut out the panels on the second sheet. This process may be repeated for deeper panels if desired. When the layers of panels have been cut out, glue all the sheets together with a sheet of plain card at the back, carefully aligning them so that the cut-out rectangles form a stepped recess. Rectangles of thin card for *raised fields* – the flat, raised panels sometimes found at the centre of each recessed panel on period doors – can be added at this stage if required.

Finally, trim around the outside of the door, cutting through all layers of card. If the paper hinge needs to be glued to the front of the door, the edge of the paper strip can be aligned with the edge of the panels to make it almost invisible. Note that if the door opens in such a way that both sides will be seen by the audience, it may be necessary for it to be built with panelling on each side. Use very thin card for building doors in this way or the model door will become impossibly thick.

Doorknobs

Miniature knobs made from brass, plastic or wood can be bought from dolls' house suppliers, and although the doorknobs made for dolls' houses are usually made at a scale too large for set models, the knobs intended for drawers and cupboards are generally about right. Alternatively, good doorknobs can be made by cutting the head off a round-headed dressmaker's pin, leaving a short length of the pin to glue into the door. Make a small hole in the door to hold the tiny shaft and glue it very firmly into place: doorknobs seem to hold a particular fascination for the viewer, and it is inevitable that someone will be unable to resist the temptation to give one a good tug to see if it really works.

WINDOWS

The method of cutting out window panes from card has already been discussed in the previous chapter (*see* Cutting Out Very Small Parts, page 62). Casement windows (those hinged to open like a door) can be made to open by hingeing them with a paper strip in the same way as a door. Sash or double-hung windows are best not made to be practical, even if they are to be practical on stage; it is almost impossible to make them work really smoothly in a model, and they tend to get broken very rapidly. However, they should be built with the correct overlap of the upper and lower parts.

Particularly delicate window frames may be

Casement window

Sash, or double-hung window

Window types.

A model stained-glass window. The coloured glass and leading have been printed from a computer on to acetate. The window is 7.5cm (about 3in) high.

strengthened and hardened by very carefully dribbling cyanoacrylate (superglue) over them, as described on page 63.

Stage windows are sometimes glazed with clear plastic, but often they are just left open to avoid problems with reflected lights. Sometimes gauze is used as a substitute for glass to avoid reflection. Check the treatment of windows in the set, and use a similar technique in your model. Acetate can be used as a substitute for plastic 'glass' if this is needed, but remember to paint the window frames before gluing the acetate in place or you will be unable to paint the edges without getting paint on to the panes. Fine organza can be used to suggest a gauzed window in a model.

Stained-Glass Windows

Stained-glass windows can be made by painting them on acetate: make sure you use the kind of acetate specially designed for graphic work, and trace off the pattern of the 'leading' with a drafting pen. Special transparent paints designed for use on glass are sold in art stores, but coloured inks can also be used, and are rather more versatile as they are usually available in a much wider range of colours, and can be mixed or diluted with

Decorative panelling in a set model. (The bookcase is 10cm/4in high.)

78

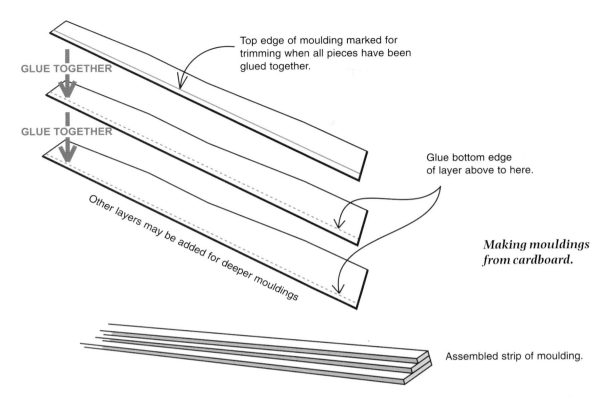

GLUE TOGETHER

Top edge of moulding marked for
trimming when all pieces have been
glued together.

GLUE TOGETHER

Glue bottom edge
of layer above to here.

Other layers may be added for deeper mouldings

*Making mouldings
from cardboard.*

Assembled strip of moulding.

distilled water if necessary. Paint the coloured glass carefully with a very small sable brush, and the drafting ink outlines will prevent the ink from spreading, confining it to the areas intended. Coloured inks dry slightly unevenly on acetate, giving a good impression of the graduated tones in real stained glass.

An easier, but not quite so versatile method is to draw up a digital version of the design in a computer graphics program, then simply print it on to a sheet of printable acetate, cut it out, and glue it directly into the model window frame.

PANELLING AND MOULDINGS

Panelled walls for period set models can be made in exactly the same way as described for panelled doors above (*see* Recessed Panels, above, page 76), but moulding such as chair rails, picture rails, skirting boards (or 'baseboards') and cornice moulding needs to be added on top of the panelled areas for a good three-dimensional profile. Use

thin card when building panelled walls, and bear in mind that the total thickness will probably be greater than the thickness of a sheet of mount-board, so you will need to make a greater allowance than usual here. This is important in order to maintain a constant width for the vertical timbers separating the panels at the corners of the set.

For the applied mouldings such as chair rails and picture rails, dolls' house mouldings usually look best. However, they will probably need to be trimmed to the appropriate width before use. Take particular care when joining at corners; use a mitre box whenever possible to ensure a snug fit.

Mouldings can also be built up from strips of card as in the diagram above. Glue the strips together as shown, leaving the final cut through all the layers at the top of the moulding until the strips have all been glued together to produce a really neat edge. Mitre the strips to fit neatly at corners in the usual way.

79

Detail of set model with rococo details. The doors at the back are 10cm (about 4in) high.

Baroque and Rococo Mouldings

The elaborately carved, flowing lines of baroque decoration, or the raised plasterwork friezes often found in Victorian rooms, need specialized treatment. Trace off the design with graphite paper; cut out any larger elements such as shells, plaques or shields from thin card, and glue into position to receive further modelled detail later. Finely carved or moulded details such as acanthus scrolls and floral sprays can be modelled using *contour paste*. This useful product is actually made for applying raised decorative lines on to glassware and china, and is available in small tubes with a nozzle that can be used to 'pipe' fine lines of the paste on to a surface. Cut off the end of the plastic nozzle very near the top to produce the finest line possible.

The instructions on the tube will tell you to bake the product to make it permanent, but this only applies when using it on glassware, and you will be relieved to know that it is not necessary to bake your cardboard model. However, the paste does take a considerable time to harden, so leave it to dry overnight at least, and preferably longer. Contour paste is normally black, but it is also available in other colours, including gold and silver.

Special nibs are available for specialized work, rather like those used for making icing-sugar decorations on cakes. However, you might like to try transferring the paste to a disposable hypodermic syringe for very fine work. Cut off the point of the needle before use, as described on page 64.

The very fine plaster sold for casting from moulds can also be used for model decorative motifs, and has the advantage of a rapid drying time. It can be applied with a fine brush, building up the modelled details in layers as the plaster dries, or piped from a hypodermic needle as described above. (Note that this will, of course, ruin the syringe, so try to complete all the work at one time, if possible.)

PILLARS AND CAPITALS

Wooden dowel is the obvious material for pillars. It is available from as small as about 1.5mm ($^{1}/_{16}$in) in diameter. Occasionally a particular diameter is needed which is non-standard and impossible to buy 'off the shelf': in this case you can use a dowel with a smaller diameter and build it up to the thickness required by rolling pasted paper around it. Use quite a lot of paste so that it soaks into the paper, converting it to *papier mâché*. It will then dry hard enough to be trimmed to the length desired with a saw and mitre box. Capitals and bases can be built from layers of card, with smooth cord or plastic-covered wire glued in place for the circular mouldings running around the column.

Research the correct style of capital, unless this is clearly shown on the working drawings. There are generally considered to be five classical orders of architecture, each typified by a distinctive

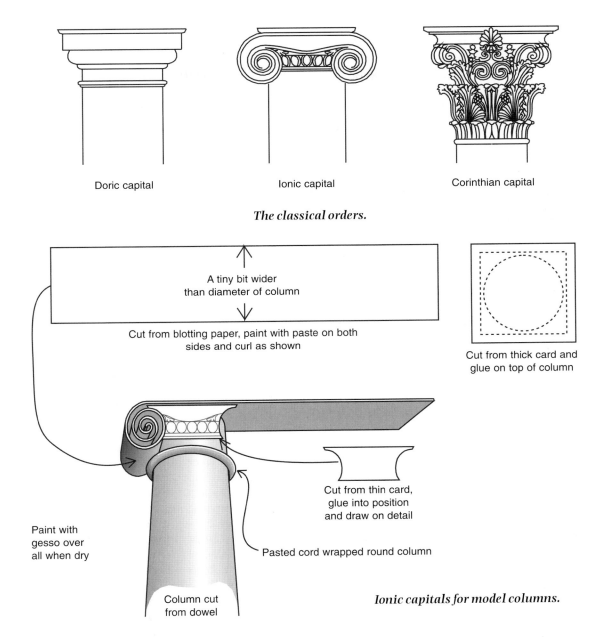

Doric capital   Ionic capital   Corinthian capital

The classical orders.

A tiny bit wider
than diameter of column

Cut from blotting paper, paint with paste on both
sides and curl as shown

Cut from thick card and
glue on top of column

Cut from thin card,
glue into position
and draw on detail

Paint with
gesso over
all when dry

Pasted cord wrapped round column

Column cut
from dowel

Ionic capitals for model columns.

capital. However, three of these are most common: Doric, Ionic and Corinthian. The Doric capital is the simplest to make, requiring little more than some smooth cord glued around the column and a square of mount-board of the right thickness glued to the top. Coat with gesso overall before painting to unify the assortment of materials used for construction and to conceal the fibrous nature of the string mouldings. Ionic or Corinthian capitals can be modelled and cast in plaster as described below (*see* Modelling and Casting, page 84), or built from card and paper as in the following diagrams.

Fluted shafts can be made by gluing straight

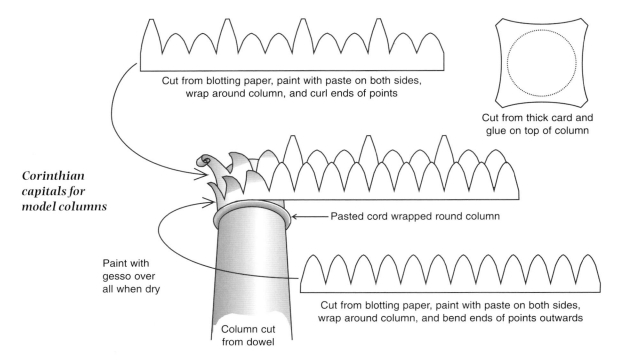

Cut from blotting paper, paint with paste on both sides, wrap around column, and curl ends of points

Cut from thick card and glue on top of column

Corinthian capitals for model columns

Pasted cord wrapped round column

Paint with gesso over all when dry

Cut from blotting paper, paint with paste on both sides, wrap around column, and bend ends of points outwards

Column cut from dowel

lengths of thin wire along the dowel, bearing in mind that you will need to use a dowel slightly thinner than the diameter of the finished pillar to allow for the added thickness of the wires. However, often the depth of fluting required is so shallow that it can be suggested most effectively by simply drawing it on to the columns with a ruler when painting.

Pilasters are simply rectangular-section columns set against a wall, and can be built using techniques similar to those used for round pillars.

Twisted 'barley-sugar' columns can be made by wrapping smooth cord or string around a dowelling core, and unifying with a coat of gesso. This method works most effectively by using a fairly thick string around a very thin dowel. The dowel should be completely hidden by the string when the column is completed.

BANISTERS AND BALUSTRADES

Model banisters can create major stability issues in scale models. They are often quite slender and delicate in design, and when reduced to a small

scale, they can sometimes become so fragile that they can be broken by a mere touch. This is an important consideration when deciding how these items are to be constructed. It is obviously a great help if the banisters can be actually inserted into the base, but sometimes this is not possible. Banisters usually support a handrail of some kind, and this can perform a valuable unifying support. However, it is important to make sure that every banister is glued really firmly into place at each end, making its full contribution to overall stability. Dribbling cyanoacrylate over fragile banisters will perform the double function of strengthening them and fixing them firmly into position.

For period turned balusters and newel posts, check your local dolls' house suppliers. You may find that they sell small turned wooden spindles which, although intended for much larger scale models, can often be trimmed to fit the job in hand. It is possible to buy a model-makers' lathe and turn your own spindles, but good ones are very expensive and you will need a good deal of practice before you can turn out really satisfactory pieces.

A reasonable alternative to turned wooden

82

LEFT: *Model pillars built using the techniques described above.*

BELOW: *Model banisters.*

LEFT: *Banisters built from beads and wire.*

spindles is to make them from beads threaded on to wire. Acquire a good selection of small beads in a variety of shapes and sizes. If possible, buy them all in the same colour, say, white or black. Spread a little glue on to a length of thin, rigid wire, and thread the beads into place on the wire. It is possible to build up further detail by wrapping thread around the beaded wire. Paint with glue for rigidity, and add a coat of gesso when dry to provide an acceptable surface for painting with gouache.

Metal railings and handrails can, of course, be made from soldered wire. Use straight, rigid wire available from model shops, and glue the railings into tiny holes in the base for stability. More

83

elaborate decorative ironwork can either be cut from thin card and hardened, as described above (*see* Cutting Out Very Small Parts, page 62), or, for very elaborate designs, wrought ironwork may be drawn on a piece of acetate with a drafting pen and glued between handrail and base. The design may also be printed to the acetate, but the slightly raised ink line created by a pen makes the ironwork look a little more convincing.

MODELLING AND CASTING

A wide range of proprietary pastes is now available to the model maker, and these sometimes appear to suggest a simple way to build any irregular or organic features occurring in a set model. However, there are some considerations to be borne in mind when selecting materials for modelling:

1. Will the material harden to a permanent finish? Many materials (such as Plasticine) are designed never to harden completely, and are therefore not suitable for a permanent set model. One of the most popular pastes is DAS, but remember that this can take anything from three to twelve hours to dry out completely, depending upon the size of the object.

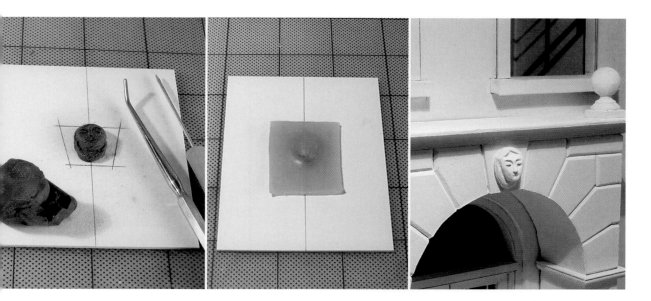

Casting from a latex mould. The head being modelled is 16×11 mm (about ⅝ in × ⅜ in).
LEFT: *Plasticine model prepared for casting.*

CENTRE: *Latex mould ready to be removed.*
RIGHT: *The head cast in dental plaster and glued in position over the model doorway.*

OPPOSITE PAGE:
Detail from a model for Twelfth Night *at the Pitlochry Festival Theatre in Scotland, showing straight metal railings (on bridge) made from soldered wire, and a curved handrail (left) supported on bowed railings cut from thin card and hardened with varnish.*

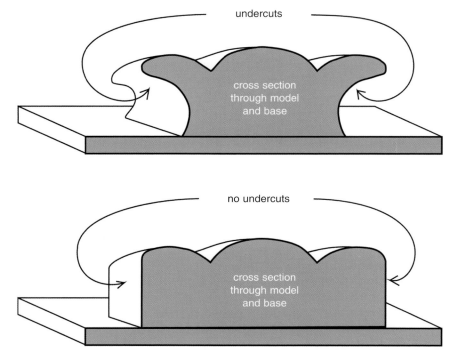

undercuts

cross section through model and base

no undercuts

cross section through model and base

RIGHT: *Avoid undercuts when casting objects in plaster.*

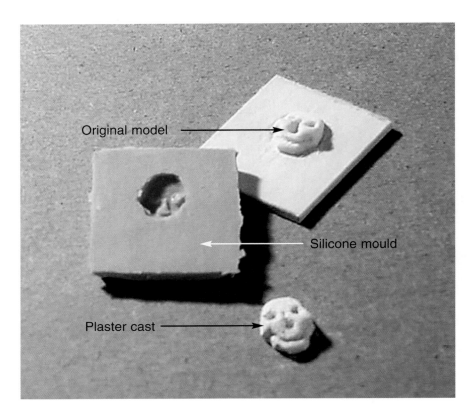

Original model

Silicone mould

Plaster cast

Casting decorative skulls from a silicone mould. The skull is 0.5cm (about ¹/₄in) tall.

2. Does the material need to undergo a specific process (such as baking) to harden? This does not, of course, rule the material out, but it could make it very inconvenient to use. Some materials (such as Milliput) come in two parts that need to be mixed together before use.

3. Does the material shrink as it hardens? This might seriously affect the scale of the object, and sometimes causes paint to flake off.

4. Will the hardened surface require any further treatment before painting with water-based paints? Some materials are wax-based and difficult to paint.

5. Can the hardened paste be worked by carving, sanding, sawing or drilling after it has set? This is not always necessary, but it is sometimes useful to be able to trim a modelled part slightly to fit it snugly into position.

For multiple objects such as corbels, balusters and capitals for pilasters, it is worthwhile taking the time to make a mould so that you can cast as many as you require, in the secure knowledge that they will all be absolutely identical. Once made, the moulds can be stored for re-use in future projects. Materials for mould making and fine 'dental' plaster for casting are available from most art stores. They are sometimes attractively packaged as a boxed set, but are cheaper and more convenient bought separately, without the sample mould of some cute but useless Disney character that is usually included in the box.

Start by tracing the outline of the object to be modelled on to a flat base such as mount-board, and model the object to be cast directly on to the base in a material such as DAS or Plasticine, using the outline drawing as a guide. It is worth spending some time and care at this stage to get the shape as clean and accurate as possible. Bear in mind that any deep undercuts will prevent the model from being removed cleanly from the mould (*see* diagram on page 85). Flexible moulds will permit some slight undercutting, but play safe and avoid it wherever possible.

When you are satisfied with your model, paint both the Plasticine and the base with Vaseline, using a small, soft brush. This will prevent latex from sticking to your model. Follow the directions on the package for applying liquid latex, paint the entire model, and an area of the base all around it to create a supporting flange on the mould. The latex changes from white to a yellowish-brown as it dries. When all the white has vanished, give the model another coat of the rubber solution; it will probably need several coats to make a really strong mould. Do not leave it for too long between coats, as the layers will bond better to each other when they have not completely dried out. Stand your brush in a jar of soapy water between coats to make it easier to clean when the job is done. When the mould is complete, remove the Plasticine and clean the mould with soap and water to remove all grease.

If you have used DAS or some other material that sets hard, you can speed up the mould-making process by using an alginate or silicone moulding paste. These are generally sold as two substances that need to be mixed together before use, in order to activate them. Once mixed, the paste will set very quickly, usually in less than five minutes, so you need to work speedily, pressing the paste firmly around the model, making sure it fills every crevice. Obviously this type of moulding paste cannot be used with a Plasticine model, for a soft model will be squashed out of shape in the process.

You are now ready to take the first cast: stand the mould in some suitable container such as the tray of a matchbox, using small pieces of Plasticine to hold it in position and prevent it tipping.

Fill the mould with water, then tip the water into a small plastic cup to mix the correct amount of plaster to fill the mould, then add a very small amount of the casting powder and mix thoroughly, following the directions on the package. Note that for a smooth mix it is important to add the plaster to the water, *not* the water to the plaster – although you can stir in a little extra water during mixing if you find the mixture is becoming too thick.

When the plaster is about the consistency of a thickish cream, pour a little into the bottom of the mould. Do not fill it at this stage. Pick up the mould and gently twist and squeeze it to force out air bubbles and encourage the plaster to flow into all the little crevices. Then replace the mould into its support, and fill it right up to the top with plaster mix. Leave it to dry for the length of time suggested on the package (probably about forty-five minutes,) then gently remove the plaster model from the mould, and leave it to dry out really thoroughly before gluing it into its place in the model. Wash all residue from the mould before taking further casts.

Casting parts in this way can seem a long-winded and rather tedious technique. However, once you have made a mould you can easily make many copies of the same object, continuing to work on other parts of your model while waiting for them to set; and the plaster offers the advantage of a good surface for painting with watercolour.

FLOORS

The stage floor constitutes an important element in any kind of set, but especially in arena or 'in-the-round' stages, and it can be treated in an infinite number of ways. The days when a painted stagecloth covering the floorboards was the only possibility available to the designer are long gone, and now designers can give their creative imaginations full rein, limited only by the bounds of practicality and budget. This means that not only can architectural sets contain real fitted carpets or period rugs, but the designer is also at liberty to choose a completely abstract treatment, or a floor made from real or painted wood, imitation marble, a highly reflective surface, or even floors covered in organic elements such as sand, earth, turf or water. The model maker will need considerable ingenuity to reproduce these floors to scale.

Many stage floors can be represented by a painted surface in the model, but pay particular attention to the type of finish required. An elegant

Three floors from set models.
RIGHT: *Floorboards painted on mount-board, finished with picture varnish and printed-paper carpets.*
OPPOSITE TOP: *Brick and stonework painted on mount-board with gouache.*
OPPOSITE BELOW: *Floorboards cut individually from obeché wood, and stained with diluted inks and watercolour.*

parquet or inlaid marble floor, for instance, only really works when it has been varnished to produce a reflection. The model maker will need to take the usual precautions to prevent warp. The importance of building a set model on to a really strong base has already been discussed, but a painted floor also requires a surface sympathetic to water-based paints. This may be obtained by gluing a sheet of mount-board firmly to the model base with a spray adhesive, first marking out the outline of the set and any details of the floor to be painted. With a very elaborate painted floor it is much easier to paint the fine detail before the set is glued permanently into position, but if you intend to apply a coat of varnish to the painted surface, do this after the set has been glued down, as many adhesives will not create a satisfactory bond with a varnished surface, and there is a possibility that the set will eventually begin to break away from its base.

Dolls' house suppliers usually stock a range of printed-paper sheets of floor treatments such as tiles and floorboards, but apart from the usual

scale problem, they often have an unfortunate mechanically regular appearance. Although this can sometimes be counteracted by spraying, spattering or painting into the printed floor once it has been firmly glued into place, it is generally much more satisfactory, and almost as quick, to paint these floors from scratch.

The dolls' house supplier will almost certainly keep a stock of period carpets and rugs that can be used in period set models, but these tend to be expensive and rarely exactly what the designer needs. It is usually better to make your own by scanning a design from a catalogue or book illustration into your computer, or downloading one from the Internet, adjusting the colours, and printing out to the size required. The printed-paper carpet can then be thickened slightly by spray-mounting it on to a piece of fabric before cutting out, and a thin strip of frayed cotton glued beneath the edges for a fringe, if appropriate.

Model railway suppliers stock sheets of flocked paper dyed and painted to look like grass, and these can be used for turf or grass matting when

needed, although you will almost inevitably need to adjust the colour by spraying or spattering with coloured inks or watercolours. For rougher grass, try treating cotton towelling with inks and paints in a similar way, and finish by brushing matt varnish into the pile with an old toothbrush for an uneven effect.

Rough stone floors can be suggested by cutting out miniature flagstones from card, and slightly distressing the corners and edges before gluing into place. It sometimes helps to cut the stones from cards of slightly different thicknesses for a particularly uneven effect. However, always remember that your aim is to imitate the set that the workshops are required to build, and if the stage floor is to be painted, then you should resist the temptation to use a three-dimensional technique in the set model. However, if a built texture is really preferable, then demonstrating the effect impressively in the model can sometimes help to persuade a reluctant management to support any extra cost that may be involved.

6 PAINTING AND TEXTURING

Generally speaking the designer will need to paint the model himself, even if it has been built by someone else. The precise colour and painting technique is often quite personal to the designer, and unless the chosen style is extremely straight-forward, it is difficult for it to be carried out by anyone else. Base colours or any flat surfaces can, of course, be painted by an assistant if necessary, but any painted textural or pictorial details will inevitably require the designer's personal attention.

The model maker should take care not to glue the model together completely before painting in such a way that it becomes impossible to reach all parts of it with a paintbrush. Some parts, particularly the floor, rostrum tops and staircases, may need to have lines ruled on them to suggest features such as planks, parquet or tile-work, and this becomes difficult when surrounding elements such as walls or banisters prevent access with a ruler. Plan ahead, and paint these parts before final assembly. Any missed edges of card on doors or window frames will show very clearly once the model has been painted, so continually check that you have access to them, or paint them as you build.

If you are glazing windows with acetate, it is essential to paint the edges of the window frames before gluing the acetate into place, or it will be quite impossible to avoid getting some messy paint smudges on to the 'glass' however carefully you work. Similarly, architectural mouldings such as chair rails, skirting boards or picture rails, which are to be a different colour from the walls behind them, are best painted before gluing into position.

Details of textured and painted surfaces from several set models.

Some forethought here will produce a neater model and save time in the long run.

COLOURS

A set model will almost inevitably be painted with a 'mixed media' technique. Most designers have a preference for a particular kind of paint, but will rarely confine themselves to a single medium. The theatre is an art form rooted in fakery, and the finish applied to a set model is no exception to this. A good deal of effort is expended trying to make cardboard surfaces look like some other material, and considerations such as 'maintaining the purity of the medium' are cast aside in favour of using whatever materials are most effective to produce the required effect. Consequently, we often find watercolour, ink, coloured pencils, wax crayons, and many other unconventional media all employed in painting a single model.

For most models, a coat of artists' gesso will provide a good base for most types of paint: it will unify construction materials and help to conceal any exposed cut edges. However, it can sometimes produce a slightly 'chalky' look to dark colours, and you may wish to avoid this. Also omit gesso from any elements built from real wood where you may wish to preserve the natural wood grain by staining rather than covering with paint.

For base colours, most designers prefer, logically enough, designer's colour, alternatively known as *gouache*. These water-based paints, usually sold in tube form, are available in a very wide range of colours, but note that the tubes of gouache in the art store are not all the same price. In fact the prices vary quite considerably: the 'earth' colours, such as burnt umber or raw sienna, are the cheapest because the raw materials needed to

91

produce these colours are inexpensive and readily available. Other colours, such as magenta and emerald green, tend to be much more expensive. However, it is always worth buying good quality paints, as they will retain their integrity well when mixed with each other, whereas cheap paints, such as children's poster colours, rapidly become muddy when combined. Try to buy all your paints from the same manufacturer; mixing together paints from different colorists can sometimes produce unexpected results.

You may be surprised to discover that colour manufacturers produce ranges containing several blacks and whites, although it seems there is little possibility for any variation of hue in these colours. However, the names refer to the way these colours are produced, their intensity, and how they will behave when mixed with other colours. You will find, for example, that 'permanent white' has the greatest opacity when painting over other colours, whereas 'zinc white' is best for mixing with other colours to produce clear tints. Similarly, 'ivory black' is usually the best black to use to mix with other colours to produce darker shades, although 'jet black' is denser and more opaque.

The rating AA or A on tubes of colour indicates that these colours will not fade when exposed to daylight, and may be considered as permanent. The series number indicates the price range, Series 1 being the cheapest and Series 6 the most expensive.

Some designers like to use acrylic paints for rendering, but their slightly glossy finish can be a disadvantage when painting models. However, they dry to a tough paint surface that works well when large areas of flat colour are needed, or for surfaces that are liable to be handled a great deal, such as the model box and base.

Range of Colours

It is not necessary to buy a huge range of colours: two reds (such as alizarin crimson and vermilion); two blues (such as Prussian blue and ultramarine); two yellows (such as lemon yellow and yellow ochre); and two browns (such as Vandyke and raw umber), together with black and white, will form a good basic palette, which may be supplemented with other, more unusual colours as they are needed. Buy large tubes of black and of white: you will probably use much more of these than other colours.

Don't forget to keep some water-based metallic colours handy. Silver and gold are needed most often, but the more unusual colours such as bronze, copper and pewter are also frequently useful, and although these may not be included in the normal gouache or acrylic ranges, they are available from specialist manufacturers.

Some coloured pencils are particularly useful for drawing in fine details such as wood grain or joins in stonework and bricks. Watercolour pencils such as those made by Caran d'Ache, which may be worked with a brush and water to soften and merge them when required, are particularly useful. The large boxes of beautifully gradated colours in the art stores are very attractive, but you will never need to use most of them, so buy individual pencils of the colours you find most useful instead: you will probably need the dull browns and greys most frequently.

The list of colour media given above is not intended to be exhaustive. You will frequently need to buy many other kinds of media, such as coloured felt-tip pens, inks or wax crayons, to carry out specific tasks.

BRUSHES

Painting models is very hard on brushes, because they are frequently used in a deliberately unconventional way on rough, textured surfaces. You should buy brushes of a reasonable quality that will hold a fine point when wet, but the best red sable brushes, made from the tail hairs of the Siberian mink, will not last long when used for painting models, and are really a waste of money for this type of work. Good camel hair (not really from camels, but merely a pseudonym for a mixture of low quality hairs) or brushes made from synthetic hair are available, and these work very satisfactorily. A good selection of sizes might be numbers 9, 4, 3, 1, and possibly a 00 for really fine work. Keep your old worn brushes for texturing very rough surfaces, and buy one or two

In 1866 Queen Victoria, a talented and enthusiastic water-colourist herself, commanded the firm of Winsor and Newton, holders of the Royal Warrant, to produce brushes for her personal use. They were to be of the highest possible quality, and in the Queen's favourite size, No. 7. The hair was to be from the finest Kolinsky sable, the ferrules of sterling silver, and the handles of ivory. The Series 7 Kolinsky Sable range of brushes is still available from Winsor and Newton today, though they are extremely costly, even without the original silver and ivory handles. They are, of course, entirely handmade, and now range in size from 000 to 10.

Synthetic hair brushes.

cheap children's brushes that you can treat as disposable for those occasional jobs that you know will probably completely ruin the brush.

APPLIED TEXTURES

Textural considerations when finishing a set model are just as important as colour, arguably more so. When a realistic brick or stucco finish is required, the model will usually need to have an actual texture applied to it, as it would on stage if it is to give a true impression of the designer's intentions. The most versatile texturing material for model work is a plaster in powder form designed to be mixed with water for use. Many art stores stock a range of ready-mixed texturing materials that are more convenient to use, but lack the roughcast quality of mixed plaster.

It is very important when selecting a plaster to note if it contains some form of adhesive to stop the plaster flaking off when set. The traditional Plaster of Paris does not have this, so you will need to add a little PVA glue to the mix to prevent it from parting with the surface it has been applied to as it dries. On the other hand, most versions of Polyfilla have excellent adhesive qualities and merely need to be mixed with water – always remembering to add the powder to the water, not the water to the powder. Ready-mixed Polyfilla is available, but it is much more versatile in powder form.

Before applying any texturing material to the model, it is a good idea to experiment a little with the method of application needed to attain the type of texture required. Try applying it with a flat hog-hair brush and stippling with the bristles for a textured stucco effect, or smearing it on with a small painter's palette knife for a less deliberately contrived appearance.

Remember that an applied texture will exert a greater pull on a card surface than paint alone, and the card therefore has a much greater tendency to warp. Any surface that is to receive this kind of attention will require stronger support than usual. (*See* Strengthening Techniques, page 66.)

A period set will inevitably contain some polished wood, either in the form of panelled doors or walls, or perhaps a parquet floor. For this, a varnish

of some kind will need to be applied. Picture varnish bought from art suppliers will give the shiniest finish. Most of the first coat will probably soak into painted board, but subsequent layers of varnish can be applied to achieve a really high gloss if this is needed. Picture varnish is spirit-based, so check that you have a suitable solvent handy for cleaning your brushes after use.

For a less high gloss finish, semi-gloss or matt varnishes are available, but water-based emulsion glazes have the advantage that they can be thinned with water to produce just the degree of shininess required. Unfortunately these glazes sometimes have a tendency to lift the paint beneath them as they are applied, but you can avoid this by spraying with fixative first. Fixatives are sold in convenient aerosol spray-cans, some of which are designated 'reworkable', which means that they are designed to dry to a finish that allows for further paintwork to be carried out on top of them, and these are particularly useful to the model maker. Other types of fixative dry to a hard glossy surface, and these

Wooden model of a touring set for **Mathieu le Gros** *in Belgium. The heavily weathered timbers were made from strips of obeché wood, with several thicknesses of thread glued along the length of the strips for the effect of raised grain. Crochet cotton was used to suggest the rope lashings holding the rough structure together.*

can sometimes be used in place of varnish, especially on large areas such as floors.

THE AIRBRUSH

The airbrush is an extremely useful tool, for it can reproduce in miniature many of the effects that a scene painter can achieve by using a paint spray on the full sized set. Many designers like to gradate the colour on large flat areas, or imitate the effect of a concentration of light at the centre by subtly darkening the top and outside edges of a set, and the airbrush is excellent for this type of work. It can also be used to reduce the intensity of colour on a

Applying Fixative

● Spray in a well ventilated location away from other people. The spray is toxic and flammable. If you have a large amount of work to spray, it is advisable to wear a respirator mask.

● Protect the work surface by covering with large sheets of newspaper. If spraying a number of pieces it is a good idea to use several layers of paper so you can simply remove the top layer before you spray each piece to prevent sticking.

● The spray works best when pointing directly ahead. Attempting to spray downwards can sometimes cause the can to splutter and deposit large blobs of fixative on to your model, so prop up the parts you are working on to at least about 45°, and never hold the can over the model.

● Stand a good distance away (about 1m/3ft), and spray in smooth continuous strokes. Do not spray too heavily. If a particularly heavy coat is required for some reason, it is better to apply two light coats than a single heavy one, allowing the fixative to dry between each coat.

● When you have finished, turn the can upside down and spray briefly to clear the nozzle. Always replace the cap after use and store out of the reach of children.

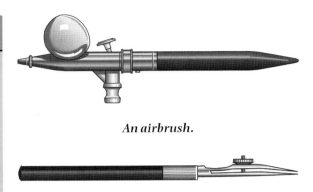

An airbrush.

Ruling pen.

to buy a complete replacement assembly, which costs almost as much as a new airbrush. You will find that after completing a job that takes only a few seconds, you will need to spend several minutes cleaning the airbrush. You can do this by spraying a quantity of clean water through it, but it is worth buying a bottle of the special solvent designed for this purpose to be certain that the brush is thoroughly clean.

Obviously you will need an air supply to use an airbrush, and although cans of compressed air are sold specifically for this purpose, it is far more economical to invest in a small compressor. Most of the air in a can will be used simply for cleaning the brush.

RULING PEN

This very useful instrument is frequently overlooked. You can buy the pens separately, but if you have bought a boxed compass set you may find you already have one, although you might have wondered what it is for and why it is included with your compasses. It is, in fact, a simple drafting pen that can be fitted into the arm of a pair of compasses for drawing ink circles. However, it can also be used for drawing lines of virtually any thickness with coloured inks, diluted gouache, watercolour or metallic paints. It is excellent for ruling very thin highlights or fine gold lines on period mouldings and around panels. (*See* below, Painted Surfaces.)

painted model by lightly spraying with a neutral grey tone. Three-dimensional textural effects can be emphasized by airbrushing across the textured surface from one side with a dark tone, so that the uneven surface of the applied texture is dramatically increased. A complementary light tone can be sprayed from the opposite side to emphasize the effect even further if desired.

Coloured inks, thinned gouache or watercolour can all be used with an airbrush, but the colours specially designed for this type of work are by far the best. They are mixed to just the right consistency, and are sold in handy bottles with a 'dropper' in the cap for ease of use.

An airbrush is an expensive and sensitive piece of equipment that needs to be carefully maintained. The needle and nozzle are carefully matched at the factory, so if any part becomes clogged you will have

Painted surface textures.

obviously running across the joins in the slabs were disguised with more colour applied up to the line. Thin, dark veining lines were drawn with an aquarelle pencil, watered slightly for a more natural look; white veining was added with permanent white gouache using a very thin brush, making the lines appear to grow naturally from light areas in the background texture, and taking care to stop them at the joins between tiles. Finally, two coats of high gloss varnish were applied for a very shiny, reflective surface.

The stone slabs at bottom left were also based with two or three colours blended together to give an uneven texture. The joins between slabs were drawn on with a dark watercolour pencil, and the texture adjusted, to avoid any obvious streaks of texture running across the join between adjacent slabs. Special attention was given to the corners, where sharp right angles would naturally become worn and slightly rounded. Some stones were given a thin colour wash to make them appear to be a slightly different colour from their neighbours, and a thin highlight was painted here and there to increase the *trompe l'oeil* effect. A matte varnish was used to heighten contrasts, intensify textures and preserve the painted surface.

Three wallpapers from set models.

The painted iron surface at bottom right was created by rubbing graphite from a 6B pencil over a dark base of Payne's grey. Rivets were suggested with a small silver highlight, and a thin, complementary shadow painted beneath it in black gouache. A mid-gloss glaze was used to prevent the graphite from rubbing off.

When reproducing textured effects with water-based paints such as gouache, you may notice a tendency for the painted surface to lose some of its brilliancy as the paint dries; sometimes, especially when the paint mix contains a considerable amount of white, it can produce a dull, rather chalky effect. This can be counteracted with a coat of matte glaze or varnish, which will restore the appearance the paint had when wet, and give some protection to the surface at the same time. However, bear in mind that some adhesives may not bond effectively with a varnished surface.

Gold and silver work best in small amounts, and most frequently need to be applied to small decorative details with a sable brush, or drawn with a ruling pen and straight-edge. Larger areas of metallic surfaces are best applied over a dark gouache or acrylic base coat. A deep olive green works well under gold, and black or dark grey provides a good base for silver. When painting large areas with metallic paints, it is a good idea to use two tones of the metallic colour if available, first applying a thin, slightly transparent coat of the darker tone, then finishing with the lighter colour, texturing slightly by dabbing the brush and keeping away from edges and corners to suggest the effect of light hitting the metal surface. Finish with a coat of gloss varnish. If rust or dirt effects are required, they are best applied on top of the varnish to break the reflective surface.

WALLPAPERS

Real wallpapers are rarely used on stage. They are generally far too pale and insipid to be really effective, and it is almost impossible to find the precise colour required, especially when it is needed to establish the atmosphere of a particular period. For this reason, wallpaper patterns are usually specially designed and painted directly on to the set by scene painters using stencil techniques. When skilfully executed, this method can be remarkably effective, and means that the designer can design exactly the pattern and colour desired. It also means that the designer can choose to have wallpaper suggested in a non-realistic style if this is preferred.

There are many books on interior design containing pictures of almost every kind of wall covering imaginable, from the very earliest examples to the present day. However, often less stylish patterns are needed on stage, and wallpaper sample books can be invaluable here: even if they do not contain exactly the pattern you require, they can provide the basic elements of a design that can be easily adapted, enlarged and re-coloured in any way desired. Computer techniques are a big help here: using your favourite graphic software, it is a simple matter to scan a pattern directly from the reference book to your computer, taking care not to infringe copyright restrictions, and make whatever adjustments are necessary. It is worth spending a little time to establish the correct pattern repeat: if this is worked out correctly, then reproducing the pattern by any technique is a simple matter, but if errors are made here, a good deal of time may be wasted at a later stage, trying to conceal resulting inaccuracies in the pattern. It is easier to work solely in outline at this stage; colour can be added later.

Help the scene painters by designing a pattern that lends itself well to reproduction by stencil, eliminating any very delicate areas that might produce a weak stencil. You will find the end result more satisfactory if these issues are dealt with at this stage, rather than left until the set is in the paint shop. Trace the outline of the repeating pattern, either by hand using tracing paper, or digitally with a computer graphics program. A vector-based program such as CorelDraw or AutoCAD is best for this, as the drawing can be expanded to any size without it disintegrating into large 'blocky' pixels. (*See* page 129.)

You can print out or photocopy A4 sheets of the wallpaper pattern to be spray-mounted to the model and painted by hand using a very small brush; or alternatively, colour the pattern digitally and print out ready-coloured sheets for use in the same way. Sometimes the less mechanical feel of a hand-painted wallpaper can be more effective, but in either case, wallpapers on stage usually look more effective with a little subtle blending, darkening areas away from the apparent source of light and lightening those facing towards it.

A slight darkening towards the top is also effective, imitating the effect of light concentrated on the lower part of the set. The easiest and most effective way to produce this effect in a set model is with an airbrush (*see* page 94), and scene painters can reproduce these effects in the paint shop using a paint spray. The miniature wallpaper pattern can be enlarged and used as a template for cutting the full-size stencil, thus ensuring that the design on the finished set is exactly as shown in the scale model.

Adapting a pattern for reproduction by stencil.
ABOVE LEFT: *Researched pattern reference.*
ABOVE RIGHT: *Pattern traced from reference, simplified and adapted for reproduction by stencil.*
BELOW LEFT: *Pattern in pink over purple background for a heavy Victorian wallpaper.*
BELOW RIGHT: *Brocade effect produced by stencilling over a gradated background, changing the pattern colour from light to dark in contrast to the tone of the background beneath it.*

7 FURNITURE AND DRESSINGS

Having completed a set model with only the furniture and dressing remaining to be built, you may feel that the bulk of your work is done. However, model furniture can take an inordinate amount of time to build, and a furnished set cannot be considered complete without at least the main pieces. Apart from other considerations, they perform a practical function similar to a scale figure, by instantly establishing the scale of the model in the mind of the viewer. Do not underestimate the time required to make them: they may be the smallest pieces, but they contain small, finicky details and need a good deal of careful work to attain a good finish. It is inevitable that the model furniture and dressings will be left until last, but you should try to allow as much time as you can spare to work on them, for if they are rushed and carelessly made they can let down the whole appearance of your model.

Some pieces of furniture may be built into the set, in which case they will probably be included in the technical drawings, just as any other elements of the set, so can be built directly from the drawings. Other furniture may be drawn from a theatre's stock, in which case you can measure and photograph the actual pieces and make scale drawings to work from. However, you will have to produce many model pieces long before the actual furniture has been found, hired or bought, and in this case you will probably need to find some suitable reference material. Some books on antique furniture contain dimensioned drawings, and these are obviously extremely useful to the model maker. Museums such as the Victoria and Albert in

The furniture for **What the Butler Saw** *is being finished with a coat of varnish before being added to the set model.*

London's South Kensington contain wonderful collections of period furniture, and are well worth visiting. Often you will be permitted to take your own photographs, but if not, all the major museums offer photographs of pieces in their collections for sale. If you don't find the ones you want in the museum shop, contact the photographic department, which will usually be able to sell you prints from their archives.

For modern furniture, catalogues from firms such as Habitat or Ikea specify dimensions of the pieces in the photographs, and these can form a very useful guide. When making any furniture it will probably save time in the long run to make a scale drawing of the piece you are building before you begin: ill-matched proportions become very obvious in a scale model. Do not spend too much time trying to include every tiny detail of elaborate decoration in a piece of furniture: the gentle taper to the legs, and the way they connect to the top of a period table, for example, are much more important to the overall appearance than, say, an over-large and clumsy-looking carved rose that would be better simply drawn on to the piece with coloured pencils.

Do not attempt to make scale furniture from balsa wood; it is far too soft and coarse-textured for such detailed work. Obeché or bass wood is far better. Tabletops are usually best cut from mountboard, to avoid the rather rough end-grain of wood showing at the edges. Glue the legs on very firmly, remembering that the furniture will almost certainly be handled a good deal when working with the model. Look at the way the legs of real tables and chairs are attached, and note what measures are employed to make them secure: you hardly ever see a table with legs attached directly to the top, for instance – there is usually a sturdy

103

Scale furniture hand-made from cardboard and obeché wood.

supporting framework underneath that offers a good fixing for the legs at each corner. The use of this commonplace technique will also make your scale models stronger and better looking. Similarly, when making model chairs, the horizontal spacers between legs are not only stylistic elements, but are also important structural features that will add considerable strength to your models.

When making model furniture, the thickness of the card you use is particularly important: mount-board is usually about 2mm (¹/₁₆in) thick. So when working at a scale of 1:25, mount-board represents a thickness of about 5cm (2in) at full size, and as this is often thicker than the wood used to make furniture, you will probably need to find a thinner card for parts where the thickness is apparent, to prevent your model furniture looking clumsy and out of scale. The visible edges of card when joined at corners also become more significant on scale furniture, so either carefully bevel pieces at the corners, or cover the sides with glued paper where needed to conceal butt joints.

Shiny or polished pieces are best left without

gesso, which produces a slightly roughened and absorbent surface that is not very suitable for varnishing. You may need to add several coats of picture varnish to wood or card to build up a really good shine, as the first coat will soak in as it dries and vanish almost completely. However, several coats of varnish will also add strength to your model.

ADAPTING DOLLS' HOUSE FURNITURE

Toy furniture such as that sold for dolls' houses has only limited use in set models. The standard scale for dolls' houses, 1:12, is almost double the industry standard scale of 1:25 most frequently used for set design. Some dolls' house pieces are made at 1:24, but they tend to look more toy-like in appearance than accurate scale models. Some small accessories can be pressed into use, but the most useful pieces are the parts intended for modellers building their own houses, such as period mouldings, miniature banisters, finials,

Rocking chair from a set model (left), *compared with a dolls' house chair* (right)

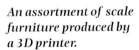

An assortment of scale furniture produced by a 3D printer.

corbels and door furniture. It is easy to cut down the wooden mouldings and spindles to the size required, and the knobs sold for drawers and cupboards are often perfect for doors at the smaller scale of set models.

Look out for cheap, small-scale, plastic room sets that can be useful for trying out arrangements of furniture in sketch models.

MODEL FURNITURE FROM A 3D PRINTER

Chapter 10 describes some digital techniques available to designers to produce computer-generated images of their work, and the use of a 3D printer to produce physical models from the computerized designs. A 3D printer has size limitations when

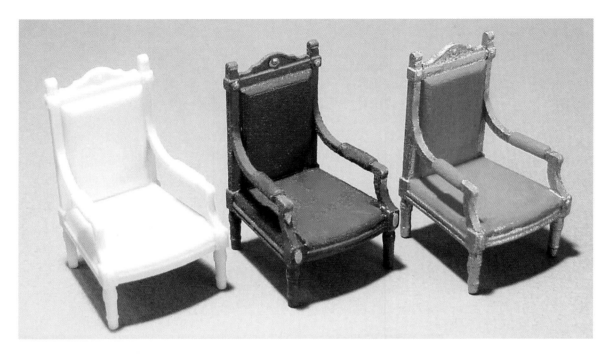

used for set models, but can be extremely useful for making scale furniture. Although 3D printers are able to produce models in full colour, it is still preferable for most purposes to use hand-colouring techniques, which offer the designer a higher degree of control and the ability to match colours exactly to those used in the set model when this is desired.

The output from the 3D printer suffers from a slightly textured surface, visible in the unpainted models in the above photograph. They also tend to be distressingly fragile, particularly those with very thin legs and spindles. A proprietary strengthening liquid is available from the manufacturers, but any superglue containing cyanoacrylate is equally effective and can be bought from any model shop. Carefully support the model with pins or thin lengths of wire over a small disposable plastic container, or hold it with tweezers or angle-nosed pliers, and dribble the cyanoacrylate over the model directly from the container, taking care not to glue the model to whatever is supporting it. This might mean treating it in two steps, turning the model over after it has dried to treat the opposite side. Buy a thin version of cyanoacrylate to soak

An armchair as produced from a 3D printer, and painted in two contrasting styles.

into the plaster very rapidly, and when dry, the model will be considerably tougher. Remember that superglue is dangerous: it is essential to obey the safety precautions outlined on page 46.

Next, prime the model with a coat of gesso for a smoother finish that will accept paint, working the gesso well into the plaster surface. At this stage, the model may be gently smoothed with fine sandpaper if desired. Base-coat the model with thick gouache or acrylic paint, using only very little water with the paint. When the base coat is dry, the model may be painted and finished with varnishes as usual.

CURTAINS AND DRAPES

Do not try to use real fabrics for curtains in a scale model; they will never look really correct, for even the finest fabric will not have sufficient weight for it to hang like the real thing. Most model makers simply resort to pieces of card cut to shape and painted to look like drapery. This technique

Painted drapery in a set model.

can work quite well, and quickly dispenses with the problem. However, the author was surprised to see the beautiful brocade bed hangings in Queen Mary's dolls' house at Windsor, which were obviously made from real fabric, but draped perfectly in miniature. The technique used here was first to carve the drapery from boxwood, then glue the fabric on to the carved form. This

technique could also be used in a set model, but finding patterned fabrics with suitably small patterns would still cause problems: the fabrics at Windsor were all specially woven for Queen Mary with scaled-down patterns.

For convincing three-dimensional miniature drapes, it is possible to model the drape first in Plasticine and paste several layers of torn tissue

107

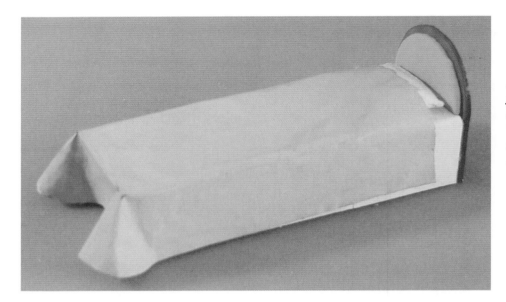

Bed cover made from painted black-wrap. The model bed is 8cm (about 3in) long.

paper over the shape, first greasing the mould with Vaseline to avoid sticking, and pushing the pasted paper well into the folds. Leave to dry thoroughly, then remove the Plasticine and finish by coating the resulting *papier mâché* drape with gesso and painting with gouache. This method can be remarkably effective, especially for elaborately draped swags, but it takes a long time to produce just a single drape in this way, so do not attempt it if you are working under pressure.

Small window curtains can be painted or printed on to thin card, with the folds painted in or simply drawn on with a pale grey felt-tip pen that is transparent enough to allow the pattern to show through the painted shadows. Net curtains can be suggested by drawing them on to acetate using a white wax Chinagraph pencil, or painting them with thin white gouache. Trim to size and glue into position.

The thin black tinfoil known as black-wrap, used by theatre electricians to wrap around stage lanterns to restrain or shape the light beam, is ideal to use for fabric items such as tablecloths, bedcovers and flags. The matt surface takes paint reasonably well, and the foil retains its shape when bent into shape or gently pressed over the furniture it is to cover.

For cushions and pillows, roll a piece of pasted blotting paper into a sausage, and cut into sections with scissors before the paste dries, taking care to keep the cuts parallel with each other. The scissors will press the edges together as they cut, leaving the miniature cushions nicely plump at the middle when the paste has dried. For unusual shapes, carve from balsa wood and cover with pasted absorbent paper. Leave cushions to dry and harden before painting.

Black borders and legs, so frequently used for masking stage sets, are usually simply suggested by the model maker with black mount-board. The effect of large stage drapes hanging in three-dimensional folds can be easily suggested by the use of corrugated cardboard painted and cut to size, but for a denser black and a rich velvety appearance, black flocked paper spray-mounted to the mount-board is ideal. Flocked paper can be bought by the metre from suppliers such as Paperchase.

PROPS AND DRESSINGS

It is rather futile to attempt to make every prop and every piece of dressing, especially for a set that is to be cluttered with a large amount of realistic dressing. Most of the small props will be bought or hired, rather than built, and sometimes an

Model demonstrating a disused, but cluttered log-cabin set.

excessive number of props in the model can obscure the structure and paint detail of the actual set. However, some miniature props are essential to give a reasonable impression of the completed set: empty bookcases in a library set, for example, will not give a fair impression of how they will appear when filled with books; gold-framed pictures might be needed to dress the walls of a period interior, and a selection of chinaware might be considered essential to complete a kitchen dresser.

The number of props and dressings to be included in a set model is a matter to be decided by the model maker's artistic judgement, rather than by the amount of time available before the model has to be presented. *More* does not necessarily mean *better* here, so decide in advance which small props are desirable, and do not be too carried away

by the natural delight in attempting a model that is complete in every tiny detail. A small side table beside a model sofa will probably be considered essential, but it might be better to exercise a little restraint when it comes to making a miniature ashtray to stand on it; and you should certainly show restraint if you find yourself thinking about miniature cigarette butts to put in the ashtray.

Ingenuity is required for model set dressings: make a collection of small objects that might be usefully recycled, such as odd-shaped beads, jewellery findings, small plastic toys from Kinder-surprise eggs, or cereal packets. Fences and other trackside features designed for model railway layouts can be particularly useful. Miniature books can be cut from different thicknesses of card, painted and glazed. Plates can be scanned from

*Model dresser
with plates.*

illustrated books on antique china or downloaded from the Internet and reduced to the size required. Glue the printed plates to thin card, making two copies for each plate. Cut out the centre from one copy, glue the resulting border on to another plate, and then cut all around the outside edge of both layers to create a slightly raised rim. Paintings can also be scanned from art books, or downloaded, reduced to scale, and cardboard frames glued around the outside edges. Remember to paint the frames before gluing in position.

Whatever props or dressings you decide to include in your model, remember that a scale model is inevitably judged by its smallest details. Very small pieces must be built accurately to scale and finished with just as much care as the main structure of your model to be really effective. Furniture legs that are a little too thick, for example, will make the whole piece look clumsy and out of scale, so do not be tempted to use wood or card that you know is too thick for extra strength merely because you have it at hand. Glue all parts together firmly but neatly, and make sure that right angles are really true. Remove any excess glue before it has a chance to dry. A coat of varnish, either gloss or matt, will soak into wood or card adding considerable strength to the entire piece, and any very fragile parts may be strengthened with cyanoacrylate, as described on page 63.

8 FLOWN SCENERY AND MOVING PARTS

Many productions require scene changes or scenic elements that move in various ways during the course of the show, and part of the set designer's job is to establish, in conjunction with the technical team, the methods by which these changes are to be accomplished. The designer does not need to know all the specialized techniques involved in stage rigging or related technologies, but he needs to make sure that his set is designed so that it is possible to achieve the changes and special effects required.

The photographs (right) show the model of a set that contains several simple tricks. Three stories by the Brothers Grimm are acted out during the course of this children's opera, and the false bookcases were designed to open out as shown, revealing brightly painted picture-book backgrounds for *Rapuntzel*, *Little Red Riding Hood* and *Rumpelstiltskin* respectively. A model such as this one needs to be carefully designed to demonstrate the special effects involved. In this case, the extra sturdily built bookcases were made to be easily removed from the model to open the hidden flaps for demonstration purposes.

Most stages of whatever type contain some method for hanging scenery and lighting equipment over and around the acting area, and purpose-built buildings will probably have a flying system that can be used to haul scenery up and out of sight of the audience. The designer will work out the most efficient way to use the space above the acting area, using a sectional drawing of the stage and auditorium (*see* page 53), and a scale model of this type of set must be able to demonstrate clearly the effect of these changes smoothly and efficiently. Do not leave these considerations until the set model is complete: they need to be planned at an early stage in the model's development to be really effective.

Model of a small set for a schools' tour of the children's opera The Brothers Grimm *directed by Kim Mattice-Wanat for Opera Nuova. The door is 7.5cm (3in) high.*

OPPOSITE: *Demonstrating a scene change with flown pieces in a set model.* PHOTO: JOSIAH HIEMSTRA

A detailed working model showing the stage machinery at the Bristol Old Vic, as it existed in about 1850. The model was built by Roger Baker at a scale of 1:12 when the stage was modernized and extended in 1972. It includes working traps, a grid with drums and pulleys, and a sliding groove system for supporting and changing painted wing pieces. The structure of the building around the stage is built from clear perspex to allow the machinery to be inspected from all sides.

PHOTO: ANDREW STOCKER

Rolling and Tumbling

These are methods used to raise backcloths out of sight of the audience when there is not enough height above the stage to fly them out with a single, straight lift.

A *roller cloth* is one specially rigged to be raised by wrapping it around a long roller rather like a giant window blind operated by ropes and pulleys from offstage.

A *tumbler* is a cloth hung from a set of flying lines in the usual manner, but with a second set of lines attached to the bottom of the cloth, so that when the cloth is raised, the bottom can also be lifted, thus virtually folding the cloth in half when in its 'out' position.

FLYING SCENERY

In the foyer of Bristol Old Vic theatre there is a glass case containing a wonderful working model of the stage machinery that was installed in the theatre in the seventeenth century. However, the set model maker is not expected to go to these extreme lengths to demonstrate scene changes in a set model. You do not need to model the entire flying system to show that a piece of scenery is flown in or out, but merely construct a simple method to demonstrate the effect to be achieved. This usually means building some form of supporting structure at the sides of the model, so that scenic elements can be hung from rods spanning the model box and suspended in the correct positions. They can then be removed to

Set model with painted cloths.

demon-strate a set change by simply lifting them clear of the model on the rods they hang from.

In theatres with limited height above the stage, certain special techniques such as *tumbling* or *roller cloths* are sometimes employed to raise backcloths or other large pieces of scenery completely out of sight. It is not necessary to make cloths that actually roll or 'tumble' in a set model, but you should include any borders or other masking indicated in the drawings. Check the height of borders from the stage, and make sure they are the same height in the model as in the sectional drawing. The precise positions of these elements are crucial for the lighting designer when plotting the positions of luminaires (stage lights).

The designer will probably produce designs for painted cloths and gauzes on card or illustration board, and these can be scanned or colour-photocopied for the model, thus leaving the original designs undamaged for use by the scene

painters. Spray-mount the copies of the designs on to mount-board to keep them flat, and make sure it is easy to set them into their correct positions in the model. Cut-cloth designs need to be mounted on to fairly thin card to avoid unsightly edges around the cutout areas as much as possible, and tint the cut edges to the same tone as the paintwork with watercolour.

GAUZES

It is difficult to represent gauzes or scrims effic-iently in a set model. Fine black silk organza can be used to suggest plain black gauze when this is needed, but avoid the very shimmery, synthetic type of organza. Dampen and press the fabric thoroughly to remove all creases, and frame it with mount-board for use in the model. Avoid a visible frame where the scrim touches the stage floor by omitting the mount-board border at the bottom

115

How Transparencies Work on Stage

Transparency effects of various kinds have been used in theatres since the mid-eighteenth century. They usually involve the use of stage gauze or *scrim* combined with carefully directed lighting. The principle is simple but often causes confusion: imagine you are walking down a residential street on a sunny day. You will probably find that many of the houses have net curtains hung at the windows, making it impossible to see into the rooms. However, walk down the same street when it is dark, and the lights inside the rooms have been switched on, and, unless the occupants have closed their heavy drapes, you will find that the net curtains now appear to be completely transparent. This is because the direction of light has been reversed: during the day, the street is brighter than the inside of the rooms, rendering the net curtains opaque, but at night, the brighter light is inside the rooms, and the net curtains seem to disappear. If the net curtains have a printed pattern, then the pattern will also vanish.

On stage the effect works in a similar manner: a specially woven gauze can be painted with transparent colours and hung across the stage so that it appears just like a solidly painted cloth when lit solely from the front; but when light is brought up on objects behind the gauze, and the front light reduced, it will become transparent and disappear.

Several different types of gauze are available from scenic suppliers, with various types of weave and different degrees of transparency. The type known as *sharkstooth* gauze is the only one suitable for the kind of effect described above. Other, finer gauzes are used for softening or hazy effects, but these are virtually impossible to suggest in a set model, and are usually ignored by the model maker.

Sometimes designs are painted in dyes or diluted paints on thin cotton sheeting, so that the painted cloth can be lit from behind, the light shining through the thin fabric. If any areas of the design are painted in thick paint they will be revealed in silhouette against the transparent areas. This type of backlit cloth can easily be suggested in model form, by scanning the design and printing it out on paper. Any solidly painted areas can then be added by painting with thick black gouache on the back, and the translucent effect demonstrated by placing a light behind it. Note that this type of backlighting is intended for *translucent* effects: it cannot be used to produce a complete transparency, as with the use of gauze described above.

edge, and either just leaving the cut edge of the organza, or carefully wrapping and gluing it around a length of rigid wire to suggest the horizontal hem-pocket containing chain or conduit that is generally used to weight the gauze on stage. Paint the cut edge with diluted PVA glue, or spray with fixative to prevent fraying if necessary.

Gauzes with painted designs are most difficult to represent in a model. Most frequently the artwork, at the same scale as the model, will be mounted and displayed in the model set without any attempt to demonstrate the transparency effect. However, it is sometimes possible to suggest a painted gauze by scanning and printing the artwork on to acetate, or by printing it on to the special transfer paper used for printing designs on to tee-shirts. The designs can then be ironed on to

white silk organza and mounted in the model, as described above. Some degree of transparency can be obtained by these methods, but the effect can never be fully demonstrated in a set model, for it is, to a large extent, dependent upon carefully directed stage lighting.

TRUCKS AND WAGONS

These are frequently used to move set pieces on stage, sometimes in view of the audience for a visible scene change, or for some special effect. In reality, the section of scenery to move will be built on to a platform mounted on heavy-duty castors and moved either by direct muscle power, or by electric motors and/or winches. When building these elements in model form it is not necessary to add wheels, as they would be completely hidden inside the base of the truck, but simply attach the scenic elements to a sturdily built base platform so that the change can be demonstrated by moving the model manually into position. The size and shape of the truck or moving platform will be established by the designer, but bear in mind that it is not really practical to have a truck lower than 15cm (6in) in reality, or it will not be high enough to contain the castors that are to carry it. Build a sturdy base for these pieces as they will be frequently handled and may suffer some fairly rough treatment. Use plenty of supports underneath. (*See* page 67.)

Check the drawings carefully to establish if flats or other pieces are designed to stand *on* the truck, or to be fixed to the *side* of the truck. This will obviously affect the height of the flats, and particularly any doorways that may be related to the trucks. Precise positioning is often critical, so mark the positions of any moving trucks on the model floor, so that they can easily be set correctly for demonstration purposes.

Trucks that move in tracks set into or on the stage floor can be guided in the same manner on the model if desired, either by cutting a groove in the baseboard and building the model truck with a short metal pin attached to its base so that it can slide along the groove, or by building a thin guide track for the truck to run against on the floor of the model. The second method may, of course, offer some obstruction to actors or other scenery, but if this is the method to be used on stage, it can be useful to have a constant reminder of this obstruction in the set model.

Sometimes trucks are designed to pivot on stage, in which case there will be a metal peg screwed to the stage floor either beneath or at the side of the truck to act as a pivot point. This important feature should be clearly marked on the stage plan. In this case, make the model truck pivot in the same way. It can be easily accomplished by drilling a small hole at the correct position in the base, and making appropriate provision for a removable pin to be inserted into the model truck. Make the 'pin' by snipping the point off a real pin, or by cutting a piece of rigid wire to the length required. It is

sometimes convenient to make the pin a good deal longer than it would be in reality, so that it can be easily removed or set without undue fiddling when demonstrating the model. Mark the position of the truck on the floor of the model, so that it can be positioned accurately for the pin to be dropped neatly into place.

REVOLVING STAGES

When a set incorporates a revolve, it is usually desirable to build a practical turntable in the model also. Some large stages have built-in revolving sections, but this is a rarity, and most revolves are specially built for productions that require them, so they can be built to whatever size may be required, and in any position on the stage. This is not such a mammoth task as it may appear, for a revolving stage is really just a circular truck with a pivot at the centre. However, bear in mind that any moving platform must be built high enough to contain the castors (see above), so it must be at least 15cm (6in) high in reality, and this should be shown to scale in the model. It is very likely that the designer will want to disguise the height of the revolving section by raising all or part of the rest of the stage floor to the same height, making the total structure much larger and more elaborate than the revolving section alone: so this, too, should be demonstrated in the model.

Mark out the revolve and any raised section of the stage floor on to mount-board, and cut out the circle for the revolve (*see* page 61). Any slight deviations from the circle will be exacerbated as the revolving section turns, so this piece must be cut with as much accuracy as possible. Some slight inaccuracy is inevitable, however, and the mount-board will not move easily if the edge rubs against an adjacent edge; so when the circle has been completely cut out, another circle should be cut about 2mm ($^1/_{16}$in) away from the perimeter of the first, removing a thin, circular sliver of board to allow a little tolerance between the two parts, even when both edges have been slightly expanded by paint and varnish.

Support the surrounding structure with a gridwork of strips of mount-board glued on edge

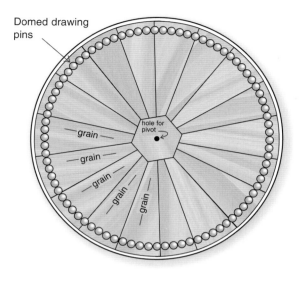

Underneath a model revolve.

beneath, as described on page 67. It is not necessary to include a curved strip under the edge of the circle you have cut away, as this will not be seen when the revolving section is in place. Just stop the supporting strips about 2mm (¹/₁₆in) away from the edge of the cutout circle.

The revolving section is best supported using a slightly different technique to make it turn smoothly: buy some balsa wood planks from your model supplier about 10cm (4in) wide, and of a thickness equivalent to the width of the strips of card used to support the surrounding section of the floor. If the precise thickness you need is not available, buy it slightly thinner and build up to the thickness desired by spray-mounting a layer of card to it. Cut a neat hexagon about 5cm (2in) across, drill a hole in the middle for the pivot, and glue the wooden hexagon underneath the circle of mount-board so that the pivot is precisely in the centre. The rest of the circle can be supported by cutting long segmental sections of balsa and gluing them in place radiating from the central hexagon as shown in the diagram above. In this way, the grain of the wood radiates from the centre of the revolve, counteracting the tendency for it to warp. Trim the edges of the balsa wood to about 2cm (³/₄in) away from the edge of the

circle to avoid friction, and leave overnight under weights for the glue to dry thoroughly.

For really smooth running, mark out a circle on the underside of the revolve at 2 or 3cm (³/₄ or 1in) inside the outer edge, and drive in round-headed brass drawing pins or upholstery tacks, all around the circle with the heads almost touching each other, as in the diagram. These will work rather like the metal gliders often found under the legs of furniture, and reduce friction as the revolve is turned. Cut a short length of thin dowel and fix it into the base board of the model precisely at the centre of the revolve, leaving a small piece of it sticking out to serve as a pivot. Slightly round the top of the wooden pivot peg with a file, so that it slips into the hole underneath the revolving section more easily. You can also reduce friction here by gluing a short length of metal or plastic tube into the hole at the centre of the revolve, so that it acts as a smooth liner. A piece of plastic drinking straw can sometimes be useful here.

First set the revolve on to its pivot, and then glue down the surrounding stage floor to the base board. Do it in this order, so any slight adjustment needed for the revolve to turn smoothly can be made to the built-up floor, rather than to the revolve itself. Note that if you need to lift the revolving section off its pivot for demonstration purposes, it will stand comfortably on a tabletop, as the projecting pivot remains in the base of the model.

A stage revolve is usually operated by running a cable all round the outside of the turntable, and diverting it to an off-stage winch by a system of pulleys. For an enthusiastic model maker there is a serious temptation to make the revolve work in a similar way in the model, so it can be demonstrated by simply turning a handle at the back or side of the model box.

The author has only attempted this on one occasion: it took many hours of effort, and worked so beautifully in the end that friends visiting the studio could not resist turning the little handle to operate the revolve. Constant use rapidly weakened the miniature pulley system, and it was irretrievably broken long before the presentation day. So no one connected with the production ever saw it working, and I vowed never to attempt to show off in this way again. You, however, may have more success than I did.

TRAPS AND LIFTS

Spectacular theatrical performances of previous generations frequently included the use of elaborate stage lifts to enable scenery to sink or rise through the stage floor. These effects are rarely used today, apart from in big musical shows such as *The Phantom of the Opera*. However, many newer stages are built with removable floor sections that enable traps or sub-stage levels to be incorporated into sets when these are required. Most frequently, stage traps are literally just doors set into the floor, used within the context of the play to provide access to a lower level of some kind, and only rarely involve any elaborate machinery. All the model maker needs to do in this case is simply to outline the door in the correct position on the floor of the model. This can be built as a practical door if desired, complete with under-stage steps.

It is not difficult to build a trapdoor in the same way as described for normal doors on page 75; however, there will need to be sufficient space between the stage floor and the base board of the model to allow room for the under-stage elements, and it is a good idea to leave access space to get your hand underneath the trap to open it from below when displaying the model. Trim away a little of the board around the door for a fairly loose fit, allowing for the slight increase in size it will eventually acquire from paint and varnish.

Sometimes a set will incorporate some special effect that makes it essential to be able to remove a sizeable section of the floor to build in scenic elements beneath the stage. In this case, you should build the model so that part of the floor may be lifted out and a new part inserted carrying whatever scenery is required. Attempting to build practical stage lifts into a model is a tricky task with many pitfalls, and it is generally preferable to play safe and demonstrate effects such as these in the simplest way possible. It is also useful from a practical point of view to have the sub-stage part separate from the main-stage model for close examination.

BUILT-IN LIGHTS

You may occasionally see wonderful stage models rigged with a complete array of miniature stage lights that work just like the real thing. These impressive models are also extremely high cost, however, as the miniature spotlights are often more expensive to produce than the full-size stage lanterns. Furthermore they have limited practical use to the designer, as it is most improbable that the miniature lighting equipment would be able to create anything approaching the lighting that would be used on stage. However, there are times when it might be desirable to build some lights into a set model to demonstrate special effects: for example, a rostrum might contain some under-floor lighting, or the set may contain some special panels with built in back-lighting. In cases such as these, the model maker can build light-boxes into the model containing bulbs operated by battery or through a transformer. Do not forget to allow for access to change bulbs or batteries when this becomes necessary.

If you really need to make lamps or chandeliers that light up, dolls' house suppliers usually stock a range of 'pea-' or miniature candle bulbs with tiny plugs, socket strips and transformers to operate them. However, decide first if these effects have any real value, and do not be tempted to turn your set model into a toy.

9 PEOPLE, TREES AND OTHER ORGANIC ELEMENTS

The main value of including human figures in a set model is that they are able to give an instant sense of scale to even the least technically minded viewer. The model maker too, needs to keep the scale of the model under construction constantly in mind, and a simple cutout cardboard figure at the same scale should be a constant companion on the work surface and when demonstrating a set model to others.

The cardboard figure in the illustration right is the one that appears in many of the photographs in Chapter 12 Constructing a Set Model Step by Step. It took only a minute or two to make, but has stood on the author's work surface for a good many years. It has performed its task with equal efficiency in sets for shows of all kinds, including pantomimes and operas, and on several occasions has prevented serious errors.

The stage at the Wolf Trap Center for the Performing Arts near Washington, DC, is extremely large, so a set model at the usual scale of 1:25 was an impractical proposition, as it was to be transported to Washington by air. Even at a scale of 1:50, the model base was over 1.25m (about 4ft) square. Consequently the two small figures shown in the photograph overleaf played an important role in putting this large model into context: by comparing the size of these figures with the wood-planked columns beside them, the great height is immediately apparent, whereas in the model the columns are actually only about 90cm (3ft) high.

The scale figures in the photograph at the top of page 122 were bought from an architectural model supplier. Human figures at all the popular

OPPOSITE: *Scale model people, constructed using various techniques, pose on the steps of a model set.* PHOTO: JOSIAH HIEMSTRA

A rapidly sketched figure cut from card and supported behind is useful to give a sense of scale.

scales can be bought from good model shops. They are usually sold unpainted, made from white plaster or plastic, and often with moveable or replaceable limbs in various positions. They are excellent for presentation work, but suffer from a generalization of style that can sometimes give the impression that some passerby from the street has accidentally wandered on to the stage.

MAKING TWO-DIMENSIONAL MODEL PEOPLE

When designing both set and costumes it can often be very helpful to scan the costume designs and reduce them to the correct scale, then print them out and spray-mount them on to thin card. These can then be cut out to make scale figures of the characters dressed in the actual clothes they are to wear on stage.

The costume design on page 123 was produced by first photographing the performer, Patricia

121

Detail of a model of the huge stage at Wolf Trap near Washington DC, USA, showing the use of human figures to establish the scale of this unusually large model.

Cutout cardboard figures made from costume designs for a production of **Village of Idiots.**

Darbasie, and using the photograph as a basis for the drawing. The actual fabric selected was scanned, reduced in size, and printed on to the dress drawn in the design. The completed costume rendering was then reduced to scale, and printed out on to card stock to make a scale figure for use in the set model. Although only a simple cardboard cutout, when placed in the set model it gave a reasonably good impression of how this solo performer would appear in the set wearing the actual costume.

To be effective, cutout figures need to be able to stand securely in the set model without constantly tumbling over. A small, right-angled triangular cardboard strut glued to the back will often provide sufficient support. The figure will stand more securely if the angle is a little less than a right angle, causing the cutout figure to lean backwards slightly. For a set that contains a raked or sloping floor, make two identical figures, one of them with a supporting strut cut to a suitable angle to enable it to stand upright on the model rake.

Some designers like to glue cutout figures to a circular base representing roughly the amount of space taken up by a three-dimensional figure. Sometimes a penny coin is used for this, as the weight makes the figure much less likely to topple over. However, a real penny visible on the floor of a model can sometimes be a distraction, for a coin is often included in photographs of miniatures to demonstrate how small the model is in reality, whereas precisely the opposite function is aimed at here.

A popular device for supporting cutout figures is a small sewing needle glued to the back with

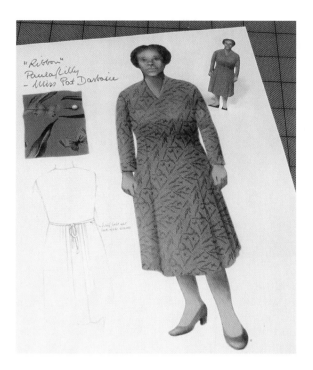

Costume design for Patricia Darbasie in her one-woman show, Ribbon, with cardboard cutout scale figure made from the scaled-down costume design.

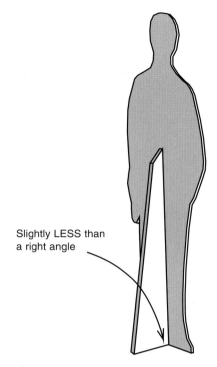

Slightly LESS than a right angle

Making a strut to support a cutout figure.

the point protruding very slightly at the bottom. The figure can then be stood up by gently pressing the point of the needle into the base of the model. This works very effectively, but sometimes has the unfortunate effect of pricking fingers and smearing blood on the model.

MAKING THREE-DIMENSIONAL MODEL PEOPLE

Many model makers like to make three-dimensional figures for their presentation models. These can be remarkably effective, but need to be modelled with great care to prevent them from appearing clumsy and doll-like – after all, the least satisfactory element in many dolls' houses is the dolls themselves: they are often propped up in stiff, unlifelike poses, wearing clothes made from real fabrics that make them look as if they are dressed in coarsely

woven sackcloth. Set models are built to a scale considerably smaller than most dolls' houses, so this effect can easily be exacerbated unless great care is taken to avoid it.

Begin by making an armature from thin, flexible wire. A doubled length of wire can be used for legs, body and head, and another piece for the arms, making tiny tear-drop shaped loops for hands and feet, as shown in the illustration. Bind them together with thread or darning wool, wrapping it round and round to thicken all parts of the body as appropriate, and bending the figure into the pose required. Keep checking the height and proportions as you work: at this stage the model should be kept considerably thinner than required for the finished figure, as extra thickness will be added at subsequent stages. When you are reasonably satisfied, paint the model with paste or diluted PVA glue, allowing it to soak well in; then leave to dry out and set.

Next, paste or glue very small pieces of torn tissue paper all over the figure, carefully adjusting

123

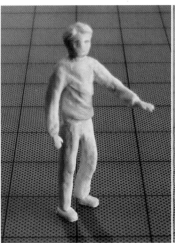

Making model people on a wire armature.

the proportions and the pose where necessary, and forming the glued paper into the features of whatever hairstyle and clothing the figure is to wear as you work. It is sometimes desirable to apply the glued paper in several stages, leaving it to set hard between layers. Additional features can be added with modelling paste if desired, but apply this sparingly to prevent the model from becoming over-thick and chunky: a figure intended for a dainty soubrette character can easily get out of control at this stage and acquire the proportions of an overweight rugby player.

If the figure is correctly posed it should not be too difficult to adjust the limbs slightly as you work so that it will stand unsupported. Small pieces of thin card glued to the bottom of each foot and trimmed to fit the foot will help the figure to stand more firmly. Finish with a coat of artists' gesso to provide a good painting surface, and paint with gouache or acrylics.

Beware of making flesh tones too pink: flesh is a very subtle colour that is frequently rendered far too bright, giving the impression that the figure is suffering from a bad case of sunburn. Use a lot of white, with a little brown and a very small amount of red added to it, and avoid the doll-like effect produced by red lips and bright blue eyes. Facial features that are merely suggested, rather than painted in great detail, will usually be found to be more expressive.

Digital Figures

A less tangible method of adding human figures to give scale to a model is to photograph the model and then add a three-dimensionally modelled digital figure to the photograph, using software such as Poser from Curious Labs. This technique is discussed more fully on page 135.

TREES

There are various techniques for making model trees, depending upon the type of tree required. Small trees on stage are sometimes simply large branches cut from real trees, trimmed and mounted, with artificial leaves added by the props department. Other trees are built from *papier mâché*, plaster bandage or some other suitable material modelled over a metal armature. Larger trees can be built over a metal or timber framework to obtain the shape required. Try to use similar techniques when building your model trees: small twigs can be selected to form the basis of the first type of tree, but they will eventually become brittle and begin to fall apart. Preserve them by dipping the twigs in matt emulsion (or latex) glaze, or hardening with cyanoacrylate as described on page 63.

The metal armature type of tree can be modelled by twisting thin, flexible wires together to form twigs, branches and trunk, then applying torn

Making a model tree on a wire armature.

Scale drawing for a tree.

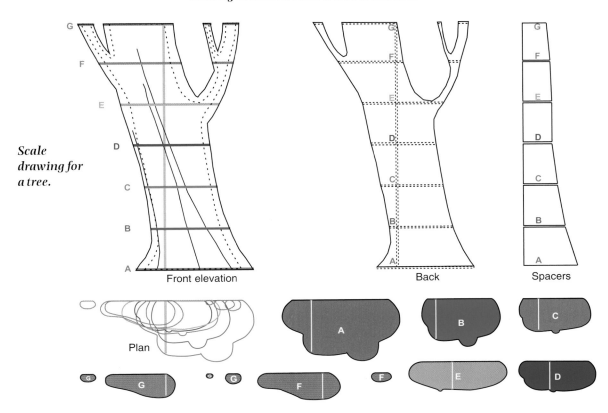

Front elevation

Back

Spacers

Plan

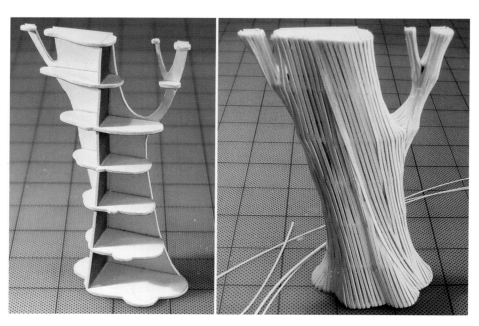

LEFT: *The assembled mount-board armature.*
RIGHT: *Strips of thin card glued to the armature in the same way that wooden laths or strips of hardboard might be applied in the workshop.*

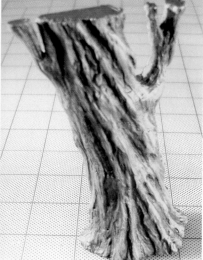

LEFT: *Lengths of string have been glued to the trunk for added 'knottiness'. The entire trunk was then covered with pasted scraps of tissue paper, and a coat of Polyfilla applied over all.*
RIGHT: *The painted tree-trunk.*

tissue paper and paste to cover and conceal the wire. Finish with a coat of gesso when dry, paint, and add foliage if required by painting the ends of the wire branches with glue, and dipping them into finely chopped paper 'leaves'. Use an assortment of green and brownish-green tones for a more realistic appearance.

Specific shapes required for large trees should be shown on the working drawings produced for the set builders, and these can form the basis for the model trees also. Build an armature similar to the kind to be constructed for the full-sized tree by cutting formers shaped like sections of the trunk from mount-board, and gluing board spacers between them. Then cover with strips of thin card as shown in the illustration. Extra textural effects

Model for 'The Home Under the Ground' set in **Peter Pan** *at Theatr Clwyd in North Wales.*

PHOTO: BARRY HAMILTON

can be added by gluing string or cord of different thicknesses along the length of the trunk, and covering with pasted tissue paper in the same way that the set decorator might use lengths of paper rope of different diameters on the full-size tree. Finish with a coat of Polyfilla or gesso.

Model-making suppliers sell scale trees for use in architectural models, but these are usually far too small, and often stylized to a degree that makes them unsuitable for use in set models.

OTHER ORGANIC FEATURES

When modelling organic elements such as rocks and trees, the model maker should bear in mind that the aim is not merely to represent these objects as you would in, say, a model railway layout, but to show them as they are designed to appear in the set on stage. In conventional staging, the set is seen only from one side, so the set builder will probably not build these elements completely three-dimensionally, and your model should reflect this. Often an uneven floor, such as one intended to suggest a rocky surface, is, in reality, a disguised series of rostra or steps, and the designer will need to bear in mind the practical consideration of making them safe and easily negotiable for actors performing on them.

The set builders will probably begin by making a

supporting structure from wood or metal, upon which the organic surface elements will be built up, sometimes modelled over wire mesh or built from fibreglass, sometimes carved from some appropriate material such as polystyrene. This may need to be finished by gluing muslin or cheesecloth over it, enclosing the entire area to conform with fire regulations and to give a suitable surface for texturing and final painting. Various proprietary materials are available for these tasks.

The designer may suggest a supporting structure in the working drawings, or he may leave this entirely to the builder. In any case, it is usually a good idea to use comparable techniques in miniature when building the set model if possible. Rocks or uneven, undulating ground, even though appearing to have a casual, natural form, will in fact need to conform precisely to the dimensions indicated in the technical drawings, and a well designed base or armature structure will help to prevent them from getting out of hand. The elements represented may appear to be freely organic, but the presentation model needs to be strictly controlled.

10 DIGITAL TECHNIQUES

DIGITAL MODELS

Digital techniques are now commonplace in a great many fields of creative activity, and theatre design is no exception. CAD software of some kind is used by most set designers to produce plans and working drawings in preference to, or to supplement, drafting by hand, and offers many advantages, one of which is the ability to produce a digital model that appears to encompass many of the attributes of a physical, hand-made model.

Computerized 3D modelling techniques were developed in the early 1970s to produce flight simulators for American military applications. They use a combination of vector geometry and bit-mapped graphical techniques to design and construct accurate three-dimensional models on your computer's screen, which can be revolved and viewed from any angle you wish at the touch of a mouse button. If you have already produced working drawings for a set using a CAD package such as AutoCAD, you will probably find that your 3D software will allow you to import your drawings to use as a basis for a digital model. Indeed, the full AutoCAD package (as opposed to AutoCAD LT) contains its own 3D modelling and rendering tools, now considerably more powerful and user-friendly than in earlier versions of the software.

It is helpful to understand two basic ways in which a computer can store and display an image: when your computer displays a photograph, say, from a digital camera, it sees it as a series of

Adjusting lighting on a digital model of a set for Kurt Weill's **Street Scene**, *directed by Brian Deedrick for Opera Nuova. Partial screen capture in 3ds Max (formerly 3D Studio MAX).*

tiny coloured dots that combine to produce the complete picture. The size of the dots, or the number of 'dots per inch' (dpi) defines the resolution of the image. These dots (or 'pixels': 'picture elements') are stored in a data file created by the software, recording the precise colour of each dot required to map out the picture. This type of image is, logically enough, referred to as a 'bit-map'. Although it provides an excellent way to record photograph images, it has the major disadvantage that when the photograph is enlarged, the size of each pixel is also enlarged, and the picture soon degrades into an obvious grid of large coloured blocks.

The alternative system, referred to as 'vector graphics', is employed to display the images used for technical drawings, or any other images that may need to be subsequently re-scaled for reproduction. The image is visualized by the computer as a series of complex geometrical shapes that can be reconstructed mathematically by, for instance, recording details such as the start and end points of a line, or the centre and radius of a circle, including the width and colour of the lines used to define the shapes. The computer records the 'x' and 'y' coordinates of each point in order to remember its precise position. Thus when the image is enlarged, the coordinates are adjusted proportionally, and the image is reconstructed using the same formulae, thus avoiding the degradation inherent in a bit-mapped image.

Like drafting programs, 3D modelling software employs vector graphics, but plots coordinates in three dimensions (x, y, and z) instead of just two. Spaces between coordinates can be filled with colours, textures or patterns, and the software works out what parts of the structure would logically be hidden by other parts and removes

129

Several rendered views of a digital model in AutoCAD of a set for Treasure Island *at Theatr Clywd in North Wales. Note the reflective table surface, the transparent glass wine bottle and candle shade. The candle flame contains a small digital light source, and the computer has worked out where and how the cast shadows should appear.*

them from the display, thus producing what appears to be a three-dimensional object on the screen, which can be revolved or enlarged without degradation.

Computers typically employ two basic techniques to produce models: a 'wire-frame' model can be constructed from coordinates, with surfaces divided into small, often triangular, segments. The wire frame can be cut, bent, folded and otherwise modified as required, the amount of detail possible depending upon the number and size of the segments. The wire-frame model can then be 'skinned' to produce what appears to be a solid object. However, although each surface is

displayed in three-dimensional space, it has zero thickness and contains only two dimensions.

For the set modeller, the alternative, 'solid modelling' technique is usually preferable. This more intuitive method employs a series of solid forms (or *primitives*), such as cubes, spheres, cylinders, cones and toruses ('doughnut' shapes) as basic building blocks. These shapes can be modified by using the digital equivalents of real-world techniques such as cutting, stretching, removing sections, or gluing parts together.

You can create your own forms by drawing a shape (or *closed spline*) and converting it to a three-dimensional object using techniques such

In this rendered view of a digital set model, the software has worked out the shadows cast on to the hall floor by the numbers applied to the glass panel above the door, lit by a light in the ceiling of the porch. Note also the light sources inside each room.

as *extrusion* (extending the object in a specific direction), *rotation* (revolving the shape around a centre line, rather like turning it on a lathe), or manipulating *nurbs* ('non-uniform rational B-splines' – don't worry about it). When a nurb is moved or adjusted in any way, the computer uses a series of mathematical equations or *algorithms* to work out the knock-on effect on immediately adjacent areas. It is rather like working with digital modelling clay, and can produce natural-looking organic effects when these are needed.

Sophisticated modelling programs such as 3ds Max are able to apply bit-mapped images such as photographs, textures or text to facets of three-dimensional images in such a way that they appear to be inherent to the faces to which they are attached.

Having constructed a digital model, and enjoyed zooming in and out and making it revolve about on your monitor screen, you can now begin the really exciting part: most modelling software will allow you to go even further towards a realistic representation of your model. Having added colour and bit-map textures, you can establish which parts are to be rough, smooth, reflective or transparent. You can even define more subtle aspects, such as the precise degree of roughness, reflectivity or transparency to be taken into account. You can also establish the number and positions of light sources, and decide upon the type, colour

and strength of each light. Indeed, with care you could simulate the effect of a complete lighting rig if you wish.

Having done this, your computer will generate an image of your model from whatever viewpoint you choose, incorporating all these aspects, and tracing the effect of each individual ray of light from its source (*ray-tracing*), to work out which parts should be in shade, which should be brightly lit, and where and how any cast shadows should appear. This whole process is called 'rendering', and it can take some time for your computer to work it all out. Indeed, if your computer has a slow processor, it can sometimes take hours to render really complex images, and you may need to leave it running all night. However, the result can be a startlingly realistic image of your digital model, which you can store to print out or manipulate further in the same way as a normal photographic image.

This ability to light a digital model in a way that is not really possible with a physical model is a great help in communicating intentions. Although it is hardly possible to reproduce accurately the effect of the actual luminaires that will be used in the theatre, the lighting of the digital model can form a useful basis for discussions with the lighting designer and director about envisaged effects and the means to achieve them.

ACQUIRING DIGITAL SKILLS

The techniques involved in constructing computerized 3D models may take some time to learn, but experienced set designers are already accustomed to thinking in three-dimensional space, so it is often just a matter of becoming familiar with the very wide range of tools offered by the software you are using, and practising these techniques until the digital tools feel as natural as your pencil, cutting knife and straight-edge.

The best method to learn digital drafting and modelling techniques depends upon your personal preference – and don't overlook the built-in tutorials accessible from the 'Help' menu on most programs. These are often a good introduction to basic techniques: 3ds Max version 8, for example, comes with a very useful tutorial on 'Working with AutoCAD files'. There are also some excellent books available for all the major software packages, containing tutorials and exercises that allow you to work in your own time and at your own pace. However, make sure you work from a book designed to be used as a *tutorial*: a software manual usually describes the tools and functions available, rather than attempting to teach you how to use them, and can seem very daunting if you are not already familiar with the software. The *...for Dummies* series can be effective if you are able to cope with the relentlessly jocular tone, but more structured instruction books with gradated exercises to work through, such as Timothy Sean Sykes' series *AutoCAD ... One Step at a Time*, or Max Dutton and Rob Doran's *3DS Max ...Revealed*, usually offer a more thorough learning experience and a good grounding in all the major aspects of the software.

Instruction books are a good way to learn if you have the self discipline to work through all the tutorials from start to finish, but if you feel you can learn better with feedback from a tutor and fellow students, it is worth signing up for a course of some kind. There is a highly recommended on-line course in AutoCAD for theatre designers developed by David Ripley, the production manager at the Royal Scottish Academy of Music and Drama in Glasgow, and vice chairman of the ABTT (Association of British Theatre Technicians) Training and Education Committee, so it has the great advantage of being aimed specifically at theatre designers. Visit David Ripley's web site at **www.cad4theatre.org.uk** for full details, and also for the freely downloadable ABTT recommended CAD standards for use in drawings for theatre work.

SOFTWARE PACKAGES

AutoCAD (from Autodesk)

AutoCAD is discussed first, as this has become the industry standard software for theatre world-wide. Unfortunately the full AutoCAD software package is very expensive to buy, but, as most designers use only a few of the many tools contained in this remarkably extensive package, many use AutoCAD LT (AutoCAD - Light). This is an excellent drafting tool which is more than adequate for most drafting tasks, but lacks the special functions needed for 3D drafting; so for digital model construction you will need to acquire the complete package. If you are a student, you may find you can gain access to it via an educational licence, so check with your college or university.

The 3D tools available with most drafting software are primarily intended to be used for the automatic production of two-dimensional layout sheets of technical drawings showing the conventional plan, elevation, sectional, isometric or perspective views, all extracted from a single digital model. The model is held in the computer's memory, and the designer can tell the computer which views or sections of the model are required, and how these views are to be displayed on the printed page. The drawing opposite illustrates this technique.

The full AutoCAD package contains a reasonable array of tools for rendering digital models, and it is possible to light and add texture to a model using techniques similar to more dedicated software. However, it has to be admitted that this is not AutoCAD's strongest feature, and many designers prefer to export models to a package such as 3ds Max for final rendering.

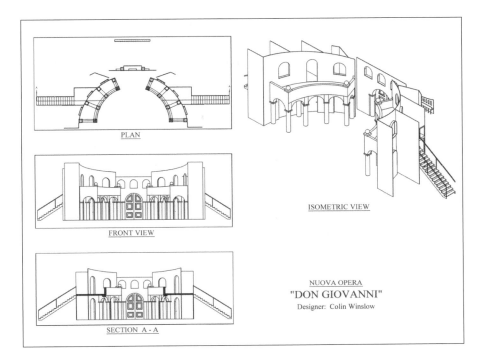

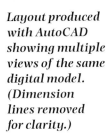

Layout produced with AutoCAD showing multiple views of the same digital model. (Dimension lines removed for clarity.)

PLAN

FRONT VIEW

SECTION A - A

ISOMETRIC VIEW

NUOVA OPERA
"DON GIOVANNI"
Designer: Colin Winslow

3ds Max

(This package was formerly 3D Studio MAX, from Autodesk.) Also from Autodesk, the same software manufacturer as AutoCAD, 3ds Max is an extremely sophisticated program with a dazzling array of features for creation, texturing, lighting, rendering and animation. Although rather daunting at first glance, 3ds Max is actually surprisingly user-friendly, considering the number and complexity of the tools available. It achieves this largely by the use of context-sensitive drop-down menus, so that whenever a function is selected, lists appear on screen containing only those steps that may be performed in relation to that particular function. It seems primarily intended to produce the kind of animations popular in the computer games market, so you may find that it has many features that you will hardly ever need to use as a set designer. However, its light attenuation functions offer a luxury that no lighting designer ever has in reality, of being able to terminate a beam of light at any desired point.

3ds Max is much better than AutoCAD when dealing with irregular and organic objects with rough or undulating surfaces, such as cushions, trees and rocks, and its animation capabilities can be used to animate scene changes and special effects, or to demonstrate lighting changes. Coming from the same software house, it is entirely compatible with AutoCAD, but also with the ability to import files from most other modelling programs, and can turn simple digital models created with other software into fully textured and effectively lit models, then render them with a high degree of realism.

Autodesk Viz

(This was formerly 3D Studio Viz.) Lacking advanced animation and effects tools, but combining many of the useful drafting aids found in programs such as AutoCAD with the kind of modelling facilities offered by 3ds Max, Viz is aimed primarily at architects and interior designers. Consequently it is a popular program with many set designers. User-friendly and capable of importing data files in all the popular formats, it has radically simplified rendering tools that are capable

133

of producing impressive photo-realistic renderings of set designs. Yet another product from Autodesk, it is, as you would expect, particularly compatible with AutoCAD.

TurboCAD (from IMSI/Design)

A popular and comparatively inexpensive drafting program, which, although lacking the huge range of features included with AutoCAD, is easier to learn, and the latest versions include 3D modelling tools and photo-realistic rendering capabilities. Versions are available for both Windows and Mac platforms, and now include AutoCAD and Google SketchUp compatibility.

WYSIWYG

(This package is from Cast Software.) Note that although most modelling software, including AutoCAD and 3ds Max, will allow you to light a digital scene by positioning a variety of digital light sources wherever you wish, you cannot look upon these lights as the direct equivalent of stage luminaires: the digital light sources in these programs emit amounts of light that are equivalent to a group of several real-world lanterns of the kinds found in theatres. WYSIWYG, on the other hand, is a suite of software products developed specifically for lighting professionals, and designed to reproduce graphically a complete stage-lighting rig. Unfortunately it is very expensive to buy, and although it has many very useful funct-ions, such as automatically generating all the usual documentation needed by lighting designers, the set designer will probably find dedicated 3D modelling programs much more useful for pro-ducing detailed digital set models.

Blender

(Package from the Blender Foundation.) This fully fledged 3d modelling, animation and rendering package with cross-platform compatibility has at least one major advantage over all the others: it is completely free. This does not mean that it is in any way inadequate; in fact, it contains many very powerful functions and offers formidable competition to many of the commercial programs. Originally developed by Ton Roosendaal as a

commercial product for Not a Number (NAN), it was subsequently released as free software, with Ton Roosendaal as the lead developer and chairman of the non-profit-making Blender Foundation. The foundation identifies its wider goal as 'to give the worldwide Internet community access to 3D technology in general, with Blender as a core.' The software undergoes continual updates and refinements by volunteer programmers from all over the world, and an annual Blender Conference takes place in Amsterdam to discuss plans for Blender's future.

All 3D modelling programs need to integrate a wide range of elaborate functions to construct really effective models, and you should not expect to become proficient immediately upon installing the software on your hard drive. Blender has a non-standard interface, which can be a little difficult to get to grips with, but help is available online, together with some good tutorials. A complete guide to the program written by Ton Roosendaal and Stefano Selleri is also available (*see* Biblio-graphy). The guide contains some very useful tutorials, a CD with the software, and provides a good approach to learning this complex program.

You can download the Blender software from the Foundation's site at **www.blender.org** – look for the link to the 'Download' section on the main page.

Google SketchUp

This is a popular, comparatively simple, but surprisingly powerful 3D modelling program that concentrates on offering an intuitive interface that is easy to get to grips with. It was developed for use primarily in the conceptual stages of design, and will enable you to build and modify models merely by dragging with the mouse rather than typing in co-ordinates as expected by more sophisticated programs. SketchUp's three-dimensional hand-sketching techniques are remarkably effective for orthogonal volumetric objects, but rather less effective when deviating from this.

You can download a free version of SketchUp at **www.sketchup.com**, but if you want to ex-port models to other formats to use in programs such as AutoCAD and 3ds Max, or use the

Rendering of computer-generated model with imported Poser figure.

lay-out tools to create pages of technical drawings or screen-based presentations, you will need to buy Google SketchUp Pro. You can find it at **www.sketchup.google.com/gsu6/buy.html**, which includes free email technical support for two years after purchase.

Poser

(A package from Curious Labs.) This software is designed specifically for the creation and animation of three-dimensional human and animal figures. It is considerably easier to learn than programs such as AutoCAD or 3ds Max, although it employs a non-standard interface that can be a little disconcerting at first sight. The software comes with a good selection of different body types, hairstyles, clothing and pre-defined poses, and the user is presented with a set of easy-to-operate tools to adjust every aspect of these stock features.

You can adjust any of the physical proportions or poses of the figures on your screen in any way, usually with a simple click and move of the mouse; you can even animate the face to make the figures speak if you wish. Items of clothing can be adjusted in a similar manner, and linked to the figure wearing them so that the clothing automatically adjusts itself when the pose is changed. Often overlooked, Poser contains some good tools for designing and modifying what it refers to as 'props': these might be personal props such as a walking stick or a wooden leg, but the same tools can also be used to create basic architectural objects such as walls and steps. Props can also be imported from AutoCAD or 3ds Max.

Having designed your figures, you can then further refine them by setting light sources, and specifying direction, colour, and intensity; you can also define the 'camera angle' or viewpoint. Poser will then render your figures, adding natural-looking shadows and textures. You can also include a pictorial background image, such as a photograph of a set model, if you wish. When you are satisfied, you can either save your rendered image as a two-dimensional picture (*.jpg*, *.tiff* etc.), or as a digital three-dimensional model. The two-dimensional version could then be added to a digital photograph of your set to give a sense of scale, or you can export the digital model to other modelling programs such as 3ds Max to be included in a digital set model. You could even add

135

Photographing a set model for interactive digital display. The model stands on a home-made turntable, with small dots of white paint around the perimeter as an aid to revolving it in regular increments between each photograph.

a whole digital audience to your digital stage in a digital auditorium, given sufficient time, energy and an appropriate degree of obsessiveness.

The VRWorx

VR Toolbox Inc. is a software house dedicated to the development of programs exploiting the QuickTime technology developed by Apple Computer Inc., and the VRWorx is a neat, user-friendly program designed primarily for creating the kind of interactive panoramic views often found on web pages, that allow the viewer to revolve a photographic image of a room or some exterior location through 360° by moving an on-screen slider with the mouse. Used inversely, however, the same software is capable of creating a photographic image of a set model on a computer screen that can be revolved in any direction by the viewer, or explored further by means of

clickable 'hotspots' in order to travel from one preset view to another.

To use the program with a real model in this way you will need to set up a simple turntable in front of your camera so that you can take a series of photographs (say, thirty-six) of your model from the same viewpoint, turning the model just a few degrees between each photograph. Alternatively you can capture a sequence of renderings of a digital model, turning it a few degrees between each rendering. You then load the pictures into your computer, and the program will link them all together to create an interactive view of your model so that it appears to rotate through 360°, 180°, or whatever angle you have decided upon when setting up the file.

It will also create a stand-alone interactive window to your specified size, together with the necessary mouse controls, in which to display the

The digital model of the set for Crimes of the Heart, *incorporated into Mel Geary's digital model of the stage and auditorium at the Timms Centre for the Arts, shows how the set will look from the end seat of the back row.*

model. The results are particularly effective when displayed on a web site, although the viewer will need the downloadable QuickTime program from **www.apple.com/quicktime/download** to display the results. (Note that although QuickTime was developed by Apple, versions are available for both Mac and PC computers.)

The same process can be used to manipulate captured screen shots of a fully rendered digital model in exactly the same way, turning the model just a few degrees and re-rendering between each capture, then loading all the pictures into the VRWorx to produce a stand-alone interactive version of the model that can be freely distributed by email to, say, the director or stage management, and easily revolved and examined on screen, even by a user with no sophisticated computer skills whatsoever.

You can see the VRWorx in action or download a free demo version from **www.vrtoolbox.com**

VIRTUAL MODELS VERSUS REAL-WORLD MODELS

It seems unlikely that digital models can ever replace the traditional hand-made type that can be handled and examined in a real-world environment. The hand-made model has a 'user-friendliness' that a computer cannot come near to emulating at this stage in its development. Nothing can replace the simple act of physically picking up a part of a scale model and moving it about to demonstrate or experiment with a set design. However, designers now use computers as matter-of-factly as they use a pencil, and to ignore the advantages they offer to the scale model maker seems like refusing to use a pencil in favour of the ancient stick of charcoal. Most designers still continue to use traditional media such as charcoal and Conté for the special qualities they offer, but no one would consider using them to produce a sheet of scale drawings, for example, when the pencil or drafting pen can do the job more accurately and with much greater ease.

Similarly, there some tasks that can be carried out by a computer with an ease and accuracy that traditional techniques cannot emulate. What is lost is the reassuring, tactile quality of a well-made physical model. Familiarity with computers breeds both respect and contempt for them: we have great respect for the technology, but are contemptuous when we discover that among its many inherent inadequacies is the simple fact that computers can, and do, lie to us. It is much harder to conceal any

137

A Trotec Speedy 300 laser cutter in action.

shortcomings in design in a hand-built scale model than in an impressive digital rendering viewed on a screen, where we still tend to merely goggle at the technology.

CAD, CAM AND CNC

CAD (Computer-Aided Design) is, by definition, concerned with the creation of a design using a computer, whereas CAM (Computer-Aided Manufacture) refers to techniques that use computer-operated machines to manufacture objects. These techniques are sometimes called CNC (Computer Numerical Control), as early systems used only numerical data to achieve this. These systems include tools such as laser cutters, milling or routering machines, and 3D printers.

A digital model can offer many practical advantages in the real world; perhaps the most obvious is by making available hard-copy photo-realistic images of a set long before a physical scale model can be built by hand, rather like the computer-generated images often seen displayed around major construction sites showing rather glamorized views of the completed building. In the same way, set renderings can be printed out at large scale and in full colour using the same printer/plotter used to produce large-scale technical drawings, and displayed on the rehearsal room wall. At a smaller scale, the pictures can be reproduced on stage plans and working drawings as a handy reference in the workshops (*see* page 156).

However, moving from CAD to CAM makes a range of manufacturing techniques available to the set designer that can offer a great deal of material help if he is able to gain access to the machinery – although unfortunately this is usually far beyond the scope of individual designers. But they are available commercially, and many educational institutions have these machines in their Architecture or Industrial Design departments. Even if you are no longer a student, it is sometimes possible to use them for special jobs, if you just approach departmental heads.

Laser Cutters

Using a laser it is possible to cut out parts from a wide range of materials such as paper, card, fabric, plastic, wood or MDF with great speed and to a high degree of accuracy. If you are already using CAD software to draft technical drawings, it is a small step to send your working drawings to a laser cutter, just as you would to a plotter or printer, and cut out all the flat parts from card or Plastruct sheets ready for assembly. A laser cutter cannot completely replace the cutting knife and straight-edge, but can be a great time-saver if you have a large number of really fiddly items such as window frames to cut out.

Most laser cutters are also capable of etching on a wide range of materials, including glass and metal, so effects such as brick textures are easy to produce, and with the special rotary attachment sold with the machine, you can also produce items such as balusters and fluted columns that are very difficult to make by hand. You could even etch your set design on to whisky glasses and really impress your director when you offer a drink after a design meeting.

The smoke and toxic fumes given off in use make a properly vented extraction unit and filter essential, so proper installation is an important health and safety issue. You cannot expect just to plug a laser cutter into your computer and start using it immediately, as you can a printer. Other considerations also affect the cost: for instance, the more powerful the laser, the faster it will cut – so a 50W laser will work at twice the speed of a 25W machine. And obviously, the larger the bed, the

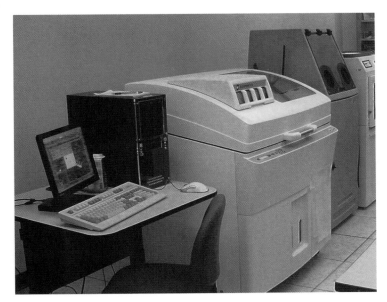

The Spectrum Z510 colour 3D printer in action. The 3D printer is the large machine nearest to the camera. Next to this is a cabinet where the model is airbrushed to remove surplus plaster powder after it is removed from the printer. The machine furthest from the camera is for wax-coating the model for an improved finish and added strength.

larger the pieces you can cut – but as you may expect, the price increases exponentially with the size of the bed.

At the time of writing, a laser cutter is probably quite beyond the means of an individual designer, but it offers great advantages to the model maker, particularly in terms of speed, and you may find you can gain access to one in your area. Check out any local firms of architectural model builders.

3D Printing

Having produced a digital model, viewed it on your monitor, rendered it and printed it out as a two-dimensional image, you may find yourself wishing you could print out a real-life three-dimensional version of your model in the same way. This is now possible, for at the time of writing, three-dimensional printers of various types are rapidly becoming more general, opening up a wide range of exciting possibilities for the model maker, although they do have limitations. The precise techniques employed vary according to the type of printer, in that some build up a model in layers of molten plastic, and others use a powdered plaster that is hardened either by exposure to ultra-violet light, or by means of a special hardening solution. The printer in the above photograph belongs to this last category, and is a Spectrum Z510 Color 3D Printing System from Z Corporation. The examples of 3D printing in this book were all produced on this machine.

How a 3D Printer Works

First, a digital model needs to be converted to a format the printer can understand. This, of course,

---

Rapid Prototyping

This is the name given to a range of related technologies used to produce physical objects directly from CAD sources. It is also known by terms such as '3D Printing', 'Additive Fabrication', 'Solid Freeform Fabrication' and 'Layered Manufacturing'.

All these technologies produce objects by building and bonding consecutive layers from an appropriate data file. For making detailed scale models this method is generally far superior to the alternative 'subtractive' methods such as milling or turning, for objects can be produced that contain a high degree of geometrical complexity, including any amount of undercutting, and, if required, containing built-in moving parts or objects enclosed within other objects. Many systems are able to produce models with fully coloured surfaces.

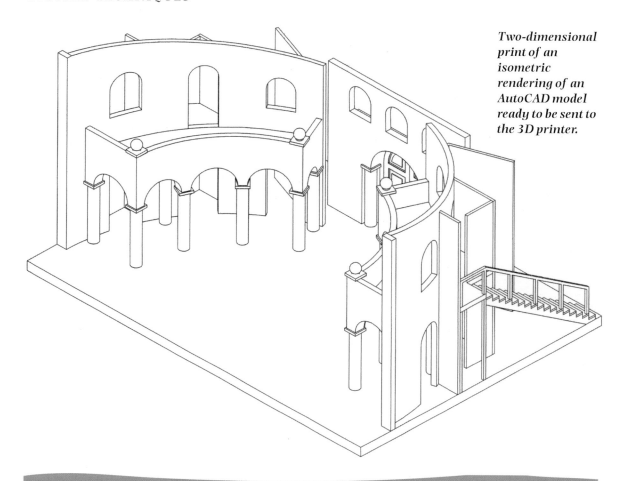

Two-dimensional print of an isometric rendering of an AutoCAD model ready to be sent to the 3D printer.

3D Printer Formats

To use any rapid prototyping device, you must send the digital information to the machine in a language it understands. This will depend upon the particular device you are using. Often it is simply a matter of 'exporting' files from the program used to create them, to the format required.

Standard Tessellation language, or .stl, was developed specifically for stereolithographical CAD software. You can export files directly from AutoCAD or 3ds Max to .stl. When exporting from AutoCAD you may find you get the rather puzzling error message: 'Object does not fall within the XYZ octent'. This means that as the format cannot handle negative dimensions (minus numbers), you simply need to re-

position your model with the 0, 0, 0 position somewhere to the bottom left in all views to avoid this. Note that no colour information is retained in .stl format.

3ds Max will also export files to the Virtual Reality Modelling Language or .vrml (usually pronounced 'vermal'), also a popular format for three-dimensional printing, which has the advantage of retaining any related colour information, including bit-mapped surfaces containing textures, text or photographic images, enabling all this to be incorporated into the output from the 3D printer if the hardware is capable of it.

Computer-generated set model produced in a single piece by a 3D printer.

will depend upon the type of printer. Usually it is simply a matter of hitting the Export button instead of Save in your modelling program, and selecting the format desired. Most 3D modelling programs now include all the popular formats.

The technology involved in printing a three-dimensional object is surprisingly simple in principle: a very thin layer of a special plaster powder is laid down on a metal bed, and a computer scans the lowest layer of the model to be printed, and 'prints' this layer on the plaster from a moving head very like an ordinary ink-jet printer, but using a special sugar solution instead of ink, that hardens the powder where it comes into contact with it.

The bed sinks a little, and another thin layer of plaster powder is laid over the first. The print head hardens the second layer of powder, welding the hardened areas to the layer beneath – and this process is repeated until the whole object has been scanned and printed. The model is now held in a container surrounded by the unprocessed powder, which is removed with an airbrush in a sealed cabinet, and can then be recycled. Finally, the object is treated with an optional coating of wax to smooth and harden the very absorbent, rather chalky surface.

The Spectrum Z510 colour 3D printer prints at 600 dpi, which is a satisfyingly high resolution, capable of defining very small details with remarkable accuracy; however, its maximum output size of $35.5 \times 25.5 \times 20.25\,\mathrm{cm}$ ($14 \times 10 \times 8\,\mathrm{in}$) is a disadvantage when attempting to print out a complete set model. Printers with larger beds are available, but a more appropriate use of the technology is for manufacturing those parts of the model that are particularly difficult to make by hand, or where a number of identical items are needed, such as balusters or pillars, rather than printing out the complete model. In fact, many parts of a model are much better built by traditional methods: simple rectangular flats such as those used for backings, for example, are far better cut from card, which is much stronger than a thin sheet of hardened plaster, and offers a better surface for painting.

A 3D printer is particularly useful for making scale furniture items: working by hand, the construction of furniture can often take longer than all the rest of the model, but once you have designed a piece in a 3D modelling program, it can be stored permanently on your hard drive ready to be printed out again whenever it is required. It doesn't take long to build up a digital furniture

Hand-built set model for Opera Nuova's The Tales of Hoffman, *including chair, table, benches and beer barrels from a 3D printer, finished and painted by hand.*
PHOTO: JOSIAH HIEMSTRA

store of frequently used items, which can be added to as special pieces are designed for individual productions. If you work for a producing house with its own furniture store, any items pulled from the store for use in a production can be measured and digitally reconstructed, to build up a collection of digital versions of popular items.

The plaster models are easy to break, but may be hardened by the use of a special hardening liquid obtainable from the manufacturers. However, a superglue containing cyanoacrylate is considerably cheaper and will work just as well. Buy the thinnest type available, and carefully dribble it over the object, allowing it to soak in to the plaster as described on page 63. Remember that cyanoacrylate is dangerous: you must always use it with very great care. (*See* page 46: Safety Precautions.)

Any flat surfaces on the printed model can be gently sanded if desired: the little emery boards used for manicure are handy for this. A coat of gesso will produce a better surface for painting with gouache, and a final coat of varnish will greatly improve the appearance of polished furniture.

At the time of writing, 3D printers are expensive and still something of a rarity. However, it is not so many years ago that a conventional colour printer was a luxury piece of hardware unaffordable for domestic use, whereas now they are commonplace in the home, and often cost little more than the replacement ink cartridges. Hardware manufacturers are currently making efforts to produce affordable, office-friendly 3D printers, and during the last few years these new printers have become much more compact and user-friendly, capable of producing a higher quality end product, and considerably less expensive.

It will not be long before a 3D printer of some kind will be a common piece of equipment in all design studios, alongside the conventional photocopier and large-scale 2D printer/plotter. The advantages for designers in being able to send physical set models around the world by email are obvious; especially to those of us who have had the unhappy and very tedious experience of attempting to pack up fragile scale models for safe dispatch by courier.

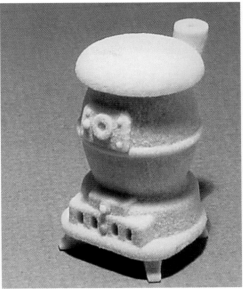

LEFT: *Digital model of a pot-bellied stove.* RIGHT: *Scale model stove from the 3D printer for inclusion in the set model.*

CAM (COMPUTER-AIDED MANUFACTURE)

The model pot-bellied stove in the illustration above, a tricky item to make by hand, was designed in AutoCAD, and printed to scale on the Spectrum Z510 3D printer. It was painted with black gouache, and finished by rubbing with graphite from a very soft pencil. It was soon realized that the full-sized stove would also cause some problems for the Props Department, so the digital model was sent to a digital milling machine and the stove was carved at full size from high-density polystyrene. The limited depth of bed meant that it was not possible to carve the stove in one piece, so it was carved in 15cm (6in) thick sections, with separate details such as knobs and feet, which were then reassembled in the workshop, painted and rubbed with graphite for an iron-like finish.

It will probably be a very long time before a full-sized set can be produced from a digital model in this way. However, government-funded research is currently under way at Loughborough University to build entire houses employing similar techniques to the 3D printer, with computer-controlled nozzles extruding a quick-drying liquid gypsum and concrete mixture to construct walls, floors and

Production photograph of Patricia Darbasie's one-woman show Ribbon, *showing the full-sized stove manufactured from the digital model by the digital milling machine.* PHOTO: ELLIS BROS

143

roofs, containing built-in ducting and pipework. The stated aim is to eliminate the need for almost all traditional components, and even to replace glass window panes with specially treated gypsum.

VIRTUAL REALITY

Although not nearly so sophisticated as encountered in science fiction movies, virtual reality techniques offer a novel way to experience a scale model: having constructed a digital model, it is only a small step further to convert it to a format suitable for display in a virtual reality environment. The photograph above shows the VizRoom at the University of Alberta, where, at the

Director and cast of **Crimes of the Heart** *prepare to step into a full-sized digital model of the set in 'virtual reality'.* PHOTO: JOSIAH HIEMSTRA

start of rehearsals, the cast of *Crimes of the Heart* is enjoying the experience of moving around in a full-size, three-dimensional image of the set.

The VizRoom is actually a three-sided booth about 4m (12ft) cubed, consisting of three large back projection screens set at right angles to each other, which the viewer enters wearing a stereoscopic vizor. The image is back-projected on to the walls, and the vizor creates a realistic three-dimensional image from the projections, which effectively immerses the viewer into the digital model. The virtual space appears to be infinitely larger than the limitations of the projection booth, and using a joystick, it is possible to move around, pass through doorways, travel up and down stairs, and even explore the back of the set.

The effect can be startlingly realistic, and somewhat dizzying, as objects that have the appearance of solidity prove to be completely insubstantial, and a sudden movement of the joystick can easily send the viewer hurtling through the virtual walls, even though he is not actually moving at all in reality. The experience is,

of course, totally dependent on the stereoscopic vizor for its effect, so it is not possible to photograph the effect successfully. The picture above merely shows what you would see if you were standing outside the projection booth.

I am most grateful to Dr Pierre Boulanger of the Department of Computing Science at the University of Alberta for allowing me access to the VizRoom. More information about the university's VizRoom and similar installations may be found at Dr Boulanger's web site at **www.cs.ualberta.ca/~pierreb/VEDP1.htm**.

11 DISPLAYING AND PRESENTING THE MODEL

Making a set model for presentation takes a very long time, and generally speaking, the most time-consuming parts – the furniture, subtle surface textures and paint techniques, and the detailed finish – come at the very end of the process. When scheduling your time you should allow for this, or you will be working on the finest detailed parts under the strain of an approaching deadline, and some long late-night sessions will become inevitable. Of course, this type of situation will inevitably occur from time to time, but it is not the most productive way to work, and you are much more likely to make errors under these conditions.

You will probably be expected to present the model on several different occasions, some of them even before it is completely finished: the director, for example, will probably want to keep an eye on the progress of the model during its construction, and should be encouraged to visit. At this stage, he or she will be formulating ideas about physical elements in the production, and the model, even at a half-completed stage, can assist with this. There will probably be a production meeting at some stage during the construction of the model, and it is helpful to have the model available for this, even if it is still at an incomplete, white-card stage. Do not be tempted to glue parts together permanently too soon, making them inaccessible for painting. For an early presentation, use drafting tape to hold pieces together temporarily, or just touch a pin-point dab of glue to them for a light hold, leaving them easy to break apart again without damage when the time comes for painting.

Finally, you will probably be asked to present your completely finished model to the cast of the

Presenting the model to the cast on the first day of rehearsal.

show at the first rehearsal. This presentation is rather different from the others, in that you will probably be showing it to a number of people with very different considerations in mind than on previous occasions. Initially your model will attract the kind of admiration inevitably accorded to any finely detailed miniature object, so you may expect a few gratifying 'oohs' and 'aahs'; after all, this is probably the first chance the cast has had to see the design that is going to become very familiar to them over the coming weeks, and it constitutes a tangible demonstration of the creative journey they are embarking on together. The enthusiasm for your work at this stage can be reassuring after attending production meetings when your design has been dispassionately dissected to discover any logistical, technical or budgetary problems, to such an extent that you are sometimes left with the sad impression that no one really appreciates your work at all.

SETTING UP A MODEL FOR PRESENTATION

When working on a model, most of your time will have been spent, logically enough, looking down upon it, but bear in mind that no one is ever going to see the finished set from this angle, apart from flymen high above the stage, so present your model in such as way that the viewer is presented initially with the audience's eye-view. This usually means placing it on a fairly high stand of some kind. 'Initially' is used here because it is sometimes useful to be able to tilt the model slightly so that the geographical layout of the stage can be appreciated. This is particularly desirable when working on site-specific or 'in-the-round' stages, where the aim is to create a performance space rather than a stage picture, as is frequently the case in a more conventional proscenium theatre. If your model is firmly fixed to a solid base, as suggested on page 72, it is a simple matter to tilt it to any angle, even turning the whole model through 90° for a bird's eye view if desired. Always remember to include a human figure of some kind to give a sense of scale.

Find out if the people you are presenting to will be sitting around a table, as is usual for a play-reading, and ask yourself how you can make sure that everyone gets a good view of the model. Perhaps it would be best to set it up to one side of the room away from the table, and invite your audience to get up from their seats and move to the model when the time comes. In this case, they will, of course, be standing, so you will need to adjust the height of the model stand appropriately.

Bearing in mind the inevitable attraction a scale model holds for everyone, you should consider hiding it until it is needed so as to avoid it becoming a distraction. A display stand on wheels that can be smoothly turned or moved into position is really helpful here. Red Deer College in Alberta, Canada, has a solidly constructed, permanent model box with convenient doors at the front of the box to hide the model until you are ready to display it. Here, designers' presentations are videoed and simultaneously projected on to a large screen. This can be a little unnerving, but it does enable the designer to demonstrate even very small details to a large group of people effectively and with ease.

LIGHTING

Having set up your model at a convenient height, pay some attention to lighting it effectively. You cannot imitate a complete stage lighting rig, but it is surprising what a great difference even just an ordinary desk lamp angled down into the top of the model will make. It enhances the colours, emphasizes textures, and generally flatters your work. A small, inexpensive halogen desk light on a heavy base with a long adjustable arm is ideal for this. Adjust the lamp carefully so that the light does not shine into the eyes of the viewers. Sometimes

two lamps are useful, the second one to create side lighting, or to light the background or model cyc. Try using a coloured gel in front of the additional light. It is a good idea to keep one or two lighting gels in your studio for this kind of experiment.

Make sure your model is thoroughly stable when set up for display. Lamps should be standing on a firm base with no possibility of them being knocked over. You will not be able to give an effective presentation if you are worried about the possibility of a total collapse caused by a teetering desk lamp. Take an emergency repair kit with you to presentations: this should always include a pair of scissors, pins, glue, and some sticky tape. You can never count on finding an electrical outlet just where you need one, so take an extension cord with you too, or make sure that one is available for your lights. When setting up, remember to wrap the cable around the table leg for a couple of turns as a safety precaution, so that if anyone should happen to catch it with a foot, there will be no chance of yanking the light attached to it, and possibly the whole model, to the floor.

You will see from the above that it takes some time to set up a model for presentation, so arrive in plenty of time so that you can do it at your leisure, and without being hampered by an enthusiastic cast eager to see your work. If you are rushed and harassed, you will not be in the right frame of mind to present your work confidently when the time comes.

THE PRESENTATION

It can be a little unnerving to present your work to a group of people you may be meeting for the first time, and who you might feel are forming critical evaluations of your work. However, you will feel much more confident if you prepare what you are going to say in advance. This does not mean learning a whole speech by heart, and it certainly does not mean writing it down and reading it out. If you are reading from, or even just referring to, notes it is impossible to maintain that all-important eye contact. You also run the risk of losing your place in your notes and the attention of your audience at the same time.

A photograph of a model taken from a low eye-level (top) can give a good impression of the audience's view of the set. However, sometimes, as in this model of a simple set for a schools tour by Opera Nuova, a picture from a high eye-level (bottom) can be useful to give a clearer impression of the actual lay-out of the stage. The model is for the children's opera Isis and the Seven Scorpions *by Dean Burry.*

149

By the time you reach the presentation stage, you will probably have spent many lonely hours cutting and gluing little pieces of card; however, this time gives you an excellent opportunity to prepare a mental list of the points you want to make. If you are feeling a little nervous, it is a great help to know exactly how you are going to begin your talk, so decide precisely what you are going to say for your opening sentence, and learn it by heart. In this way you can avoid any initial hesitation, and appear confident and in charge from the outset. After this hurdle, things will probably become a little easier, as one topic flows naturally to the next, following the list of headings you have in mind. Keep the presentation short and to the point. Do not talk too quickly, and allow a slight pause between sentences to give time for your audience to assimilate what you are saying, and examine what you are demonstrating in the model.

What you talk about when showing your model depends to a large extent upon the people you are talking to. Discussions with the director, for example, will probably be informal, and probably around your work table, so you will not need to make any special preparations for them other than a quick tidy-up. The director will require an overview of your design concept and how it relates to his own ideas about the production, but by the time the model is under way you should already be in line with each other in this respect, and he will probably be thinking about moving his actors physically around the set ('blocking'), and any actions they may have to perform that are directly related to it, such as moving furniture, answering a telephone, fighting, or falling down stairs. Point out the amount of space available in various parts of the set, estimating the actual size on the floor if necessary, and demonstrate the heights of rostra or steps. In particular point out the limits of audience sightlines, to make sure the director appreciates any parts of the stage where the actors may not be completely visible by the entire audience.

When presenting a model to technicians, say, at a production meeting, you will need to point out any parts of your design that specifically affect their work. They may not be particularly interested in how you arrived at your design concept, but will be very concerned about aspects such as scene changes or any special effects, and will expect you to explain how you have planned for them to happen. Does the show involve flown scenery? They will need to work out the number of stage crew that will be needed to run the show. Does anything have to be specially rigged to break or fall apart? Do any parts of the set come in for particularly rough treatment, such as slamming doors? These parts may require additional support. Draw attention to any safety issues such as high steps or rostra, and point out any parts that may have particular lighting issues. Do not try to avoid possible problems: they may be resolvable at an early stage, but become much more intractable if left until the set is built. A scale model is particularly useful when discussing these technical issues.

Actors, on the other hand, may like to be told a little about the thought processes that produced the set in which they are to appear; it could affect the way they see their roles. You may like to show some of the reference material you have found, especially if the show is set in a specific period or geographical location. However, they will be particularly interested to note the physical limitations of the set, such as steps or any changes in stage level. Will the steps be easy to negotiate, or will they be a hazard? Where will the access steps to higher levels be situated? Where are the entrances and exits? Will any parts of the set be out of sight from any part of the auditorium? Which way do doors open? Take care to point out any 'imaginary' walls: these are sometimes just indicated in paint on the stage floor, and are not very obvious to an actor standing on stage; however, the audience is usually very conscious of these imaginary boundaries, and will often be audibly shocked by an actor breaking the convention created by the set design and walking carelessly through an imagined wall.

Remember that although the set may be very familiar to you by this stage, the cast who will be performing in it are probably seeing it for the first time. It is important to them because it will be occupying the stage with them and affecting their performances. You have created the world which their characters are to inhabit, so give them time to appreciate the set and visualize it in relation to the way they see their roles. Avoid technical jargon that actors may not understand: you might be talking to people who have never even heard terms such as 'rostrum' or 'cyc', and they may be hesitant to ask for clarification.

It will be greatly appreciated if you are able to leave the set model in the rehearsal room for future reference: another reason to construct it as solidly as possible. If the model is needed elsewhere you can leave some photographs instead. Print out some small pictures of the model, together with a reduced stage plan on an A4 or 'Letter' size sheet, for the actors to keep in their scripts for reference.

You will sometimes be asked for permission to display your set model in the foyer of the theatre, or for a photograph of it to be reproduced in publicity material. This should never occur without your express permission, and it is up to you to decide if you wish to allow it. You may feel flattered to have your work on display, but you should remember that a scale model is built primarily as a design tool rather than a work of art in its own right, and showing the set design before it is revealed on stage, in a lighting state designed to make a specific statement at the opening of the production, might be compromising an important and exciting theatrical event. If you do decide to put your model on display, make sure that it will be shown to its best advantage: check the lighting, and make sure that it will be well protected from prying fingers. Also check that there is to be an accompanying label crediting you for your work.

PHOTOGRAPHING THE MODEL

Apart from the obvious value of having photographs of your set model to distribute during the production process, you should make a point of photographing all your work for your own personal portfolio. You will probably want to show photographs of productions you have designed, but photographs of the set model are also valuable: a portfolio containing pictures of a scale model for comparison with photographs of the completed set as it appeared on stage always impresses potential employers.

Models tend to deteriorate rapidly, so make a point of photographing them as soon as possible after completion. Use a camera tripod, and set up the model at a convenient height, so that you can see it from the audience's point of view through the viewfinder without having to bend or squat in an uncomfortable position. It is very easy to nudge the tripod or even knock over the model when you are working at an uncomfortably low level. Adjustable desk lamps are convenient for lighting the model, using side or top lighting in addition to ambient light to emphasize three-dimensional modelling or surface textures. Try using one or two pieces of coloured lighting gel to enhance the colours or light a model cyc in the same way they might be used on stage. Naturally you will want to photograph set models from the audience's viewpoint, but it is also useful to take one or two additional photographs from a fairly high angle to demonstrate the three-dimensional spatial relationships more clearly, even though the actual set may never be seen from this point of view.

DIGITAL CAMERAS

The advent of the digital camera, with its ability instantly to produce any number of pictures without the need for film, was a revolutionary innovation for designers in all fields. However, the very wide range of cameras available can sometimes cause confusion. Cameras are rated in terms of the number of megapixels they can store (a megapixel = one million pixels), and this directly relates to the size and quality of the images it can produce. For instance, a picture size of 12.7 × 17.8cm (5 × 7in) at 300dpi (dots per inch) will need about three megapixels, so you should aim for a capacity of at least five megapixels if possible. If your camera can only take pictures at 75dpi, you can still obtain good results by using a large-size image setting, then using picture-editing software to reduce the size and increase the resolution proportionally. Do not be tempted to use very high resolutions in an attempt to increase picture quality, as much depends on how your picture is to be used. There is little point in working at a very high resolution if the photograph is to be printed on a desk-top printer that only prints at 300dpi, and as the World Wide Web can only display pictures at 72dpi, you can reduce download times and save storage space by reducing the resolution accordingly.

The same principles apply to scanning pictures: a scanner is a simple type of camera, and although many scanners will cope with resolutions as high as 2,400dpi, these high resolutions are really only useful when enlarging very small images. By the way, it is not often appreciated that a conventional desk-top scanner can cope remarkably well with small three-dimensional objects. It is often possible to photograph items such as model furniture by simply laying them on the scanner's platen and covering them with a sheet of plain paper if it is not possible to close the lid over them. Working in this way, you can use a program such as Adobe Photoshop or Corel Photo-Paint to incorporate the scanned images of model furniture into a photograph of a set model if, as sometimes happens, they are not available at the time the model is photographed.

ISSUES OF COPYRIGHT

Who owns the set model? And who pays for it? The copyright of a set design automatically belongs to the artist who designed it, unless the copyright is formally assigned to someone else; and your contract should state that you are to be paid royalties if a production is to be remounted, or your set is to be reused for another production. You will sometimes be asked if you are willing to sell the copyright to a producer to avoid paying royalties if a set is to be frequently reused over an extended period, such as the set for a Christmas show or a schools' tour. It is up to you to decide if you wish to do this, and to negotiate a fee for the copyright. In doing this, you forfeit any rights you have regarding the design, and the new copyright owner may make changes to it and use it in any way he wishes.

Selling the copyright of a set design, however,

does not usually include the model or any set renderings, which remain the property of the designer. This applies even if the contract to design the set includes a clause specifying that you are to produce a model, and states how much you are to be paid to build it in addition to your design fee. The Equity Designers' Contract includes such a clause. If you, as designer, choose to use the model fee to pay someone else to make it for you, the model incorporating your design still belongs to you, and you may dispose of it as you wish. Sometimes a producer will ask if he may keep the model, and you can sell it or simply give it to him if you wish. After all, a model on display in a producer's office can provide good publicity for your work, and attempting to keep all the models you ever make soon creates a serious storage problem.

Keep all the receipts for any materials you buy, and submit them to the producer for reimbursement as soon as possible after completion, even if your contract specifies a fee for making the model: your fee should not include out-of-pocket expenses.

When making a model for a designer other than yourself, you should establish an hourly rate before you begin, and keep a very careful record of all the hours you work on the job. It is impossible to estimate exactly how long a model may take to build, and frequently the designer will ask for changes to be incorporated during the process, meaning that you may have to remake some parts, considerably extending the total number of hours required to complete the build. Once again, keep all receipts for reimbursement.

PAYING TAX

If you are receiving fees for your work, either as a designer or a model maker, you are required to declare this income to the Inspector of Taxes and pay tax on any income you receive. As income from freelance work, this is usually payable yearly in a lump sum. You may also be required to pay National Insurance contributions at the self-employed rate. Any legitimate professional expenses can be set against your income, but you must present evidence of these, usually in the form of receipts. It is very important, therefore, to keep all receipts for the expenses you incur. Some costs, such as those for expendable materials, will be reimbursable by whoever is paying you for the work, but others, such as the purchase or replacement of tools, can be set against tax. Do not ignore the smaller out-of-pocket expenses such as bus, taxi and train fares; these can amount to a significant sum over the course of a year.

Apart from expenses incurred for a specific job, you can also claim certain general expenses associated with your work, such as subscriptions to professional organizations (the Society of British Theatre Designers) or union dues (Equity), computer costs such as ink cartridges and printer paper, software, your Internet connection and rental of web space for your web site. If you work from home you can include a proportion of your telephone, electricity, heating and water bills. If you run your own car, a proportion of this cost is also deductable. Do not forget professional magazines and any books you may buy for reference.

The Society of British Theatre Designers offers a number of useful information sheets to its members on request, including one covering tax and NI contributions.

If you are working professionally and find these monetary matters a little overwhelming, you should consider employing an accountant. However, you will still have to submit breakdowns of your expenses and income to him, so you must always remember to keep a careful record of these.

12 Constructing a Set Model Step by Step

This chapter consists mainly of a step-by-step photographic record of the construction and painting of a model for Beth Henley's play *Crimes of the Heart*, from the very first cuts to the pres-

OPPOSITE: *Detail of the set model for* Crimes of the Heart *at the Timms Centre for the Arts, Edmonton, Canada. Directed by Kim McCaw.*

entation of the finished model. Many of the techniques already described in this book are shown here being used in professional practice.

Crimes of the Heart is a domestic comedy with some dark undertones, set in the living room/kitchen of an old family home in Hazlehurst, Mississippi, in 1975. It is a play of considerable charm and humour, despite the fact that the plot

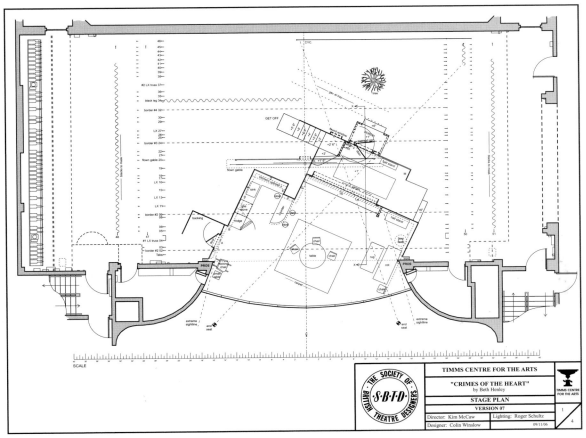

Stage plan for Crimes of the Heart.

155

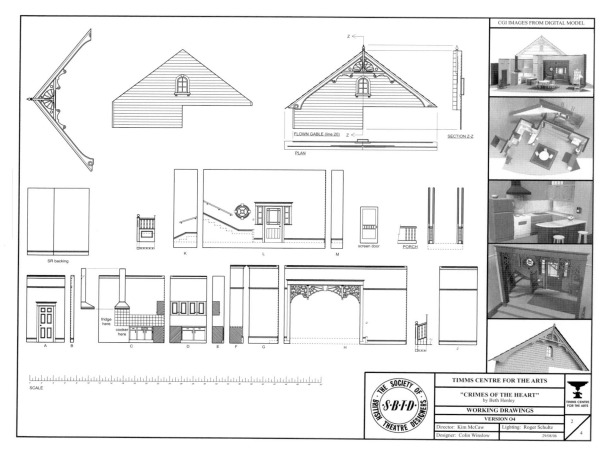

Working drawings for **Crimes of the Heart** *(dimension lines omitted for clarity).*

springs from the shooting of her husband by one of the three sisters who are the play's central characters. The production illustrated here was produced in 2006, as part of the Studio Theatre season at the Timms Centre for the Arts in Edmonton, Canada. It was directed by Kim McCaw, with lighting designed by Roger Schultz.

The play invites a high degree of realism in the set, as the action involves a large amount of stage business centred upon domestic activities, such as making and drinking lemonade, lighting the candles and eating a birthday cake, and mending the broken heel of a shoe. Ice was taken from a practical fridge, and real water ran from the taps over the sink. A touch of realism extended beyond the set with a tray of gravel laid out of sight on the

stage floor behind the set to give a slight crunching sound as actors walked over it from the wings towards the upstage door, suggesting a gravel path.

The Timms Centre has a proscenium stage and a forestage lift with a curved front edge that can be used as an extension to the stage, lowered to auditorium level, or sunk to form an orchestra pit if required. In this production the forestage lift was set at stage height to extend the stage floor through the proscenium and carry the action of this intimate play closer to the audience. The whole set, apart from the flown gable, was turned at an angle to the front edge of the stage to add visual interest and improve essential sightlines to the kitchen and hall areas. Much of the action centred upon the large table placed in the most dominant position on

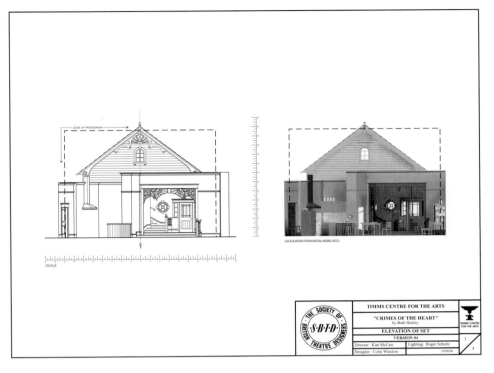

LEFT:
Elevation of the set for **Crimes of the Heart** *(including elevation of the digital model).*

BELOW:
Stage section for **Crimes of the Heart.**

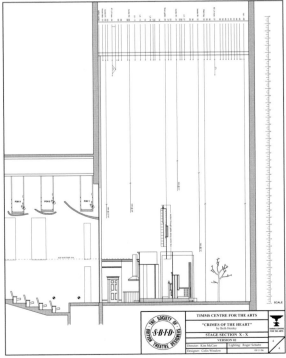

the stage, but action around the breakfast counter and the small cot-bed at downstage left gave these areas almost equal importance.

The proscenium at the Timms Centre is unusually high, and a set of normal room height would reach only to about half the height of the proscenium opening, leaving a considerable amount of space above the set, so a built gable was designed to complete the stage picture, above a room with walls of a comparatively low, but realistic, height. Although mainly decorative, the gable also performed the useful function of demonstrating the type of house in which the play takes place. Placing it, somewhat illogically, behind the room, also suggested, together with the forestage extension, that the set was bursting from the confines of the stage towards the audience, and also avoided possible technical problems for the lighting designer.

The technical drawings for this production are reproduced in miniature in the following pages, and it will be seen that they appear to contain pictures of the completed set. In fact, these pictures

157

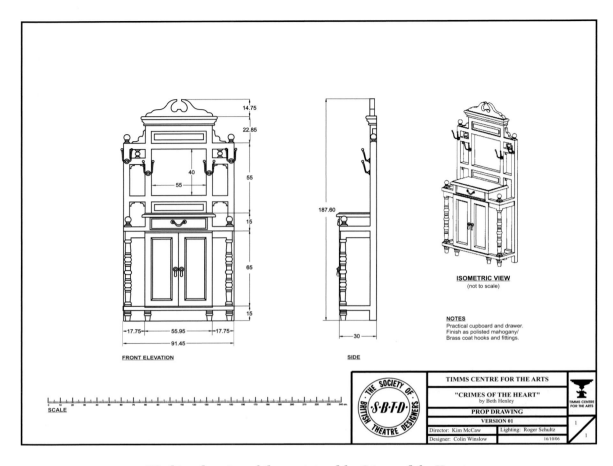

Working drawing of the coat stand for Crimes of the Heart.

were produced from a detailed three-dimensional digital model of the set, together with all its furniture and some of the dressings, existing solely on a computer's hard drive. It was constructed and rendered in AutoCAD, and imported into the drawings long before construction of the more conventional, hand-built model began.

Much of the furniture for the play could be pulled from the theatre's prop room. The kitchen dresser with plates at stage left was measured and modelled to scale from an existing piece, but the coat stand in the hall was designed and built especially for the production. These pieces, and several others, were printed out to scale from the digital model on the Spectrum Z510 3D printer for inclusion in the hand-built model.

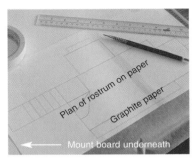

Work begins by transferring the outline of the main rostrum area from a paper printout on to mount-board using graphite paper.

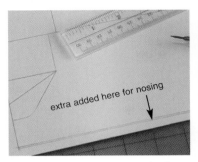

The main rostrum is marked out on the mount-board, and a narrow strip is added all along the downstage edge to form 'nosing' on the top step.

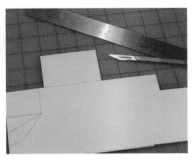

The top of the main rostrum has been cut from mount-board using a scalpel and metal ruler.

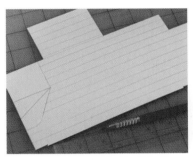

Floorboards are marked out in pencil at this stage to avoid any possible difficulty in ruling them later when the model has been assembled.

Strips of board have been cut to build the structure supporting the top, the width determined by the height of the rostrum minus the thickness of the card top.

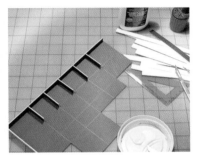

Gluing supports cut from the card strips to the underside of the top, starting at the front and working backwards, following guidelines marked out in pencil.

The supporting structure of mount-board strips is complete. It can now be turned over and placed under a weight for the glue to set completely overnight.

A cutout figure at the same scale is added as an aid to visualizing a full-sized structure instead of a mere assemblage of cardboard and glue.

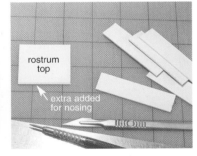

Pieces are cut out for the small rostrum which forms the landing at the turn of the stairs. A little extra is added at the front edge of the top for nosing, as before.

Mount-board strips of the correct width are glued beneath the small rostrum top, avoiding the narrow nosing strip at the front edge.

The small rostrum is now complete, and has been glued into its position on top of the main rostrum.

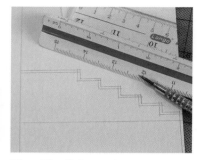

The side of the main staircase is drawn on to mount-board, with allowance made for the thickness of the board at each riser and tread.

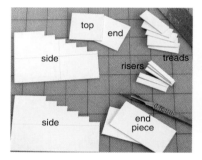

All the pieces for the main staircase have now been cut out, including strips of board for the treads and risers, adding a little to each tread for nosing as usual.

The stair unit is now almost completely assembled using PVA glue.

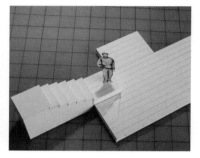

The completed staircase is glued into its position at the stage-right end of the main rostrum.

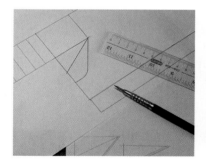

The bottom two steps are transferred from the plan on to mount-board using graphite paper, with nosing added to the leading edges as before.

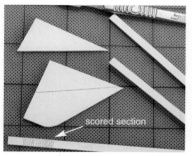

Cut out pieces for the bottom two steps, with strips of card for the risers and underneath support. Note the scoring to bend the riser around the curve of the step.

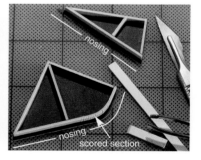

The assembled bottom steps, with supporting strips glued underneath centres. The curved riser will now have paper glued over it to hide score cuts.

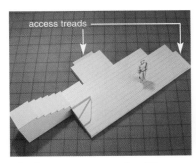

The lower steps are glued into position, and access treads have been added upstage and at stage left. These steps are not seen, so nosing is not needed.

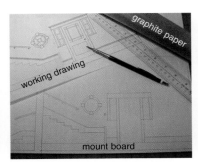

Next, the flats surrounding the upstage sides of the main rostrum are traced from a drawing on to mount-board with graphite paper.

The basic shapes have been cut out, and are tested for fit. It is easier to make adjustments at this stage than when more details have been added.

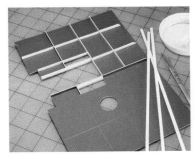

Strips of board are cut and glued to the back of the flat to form reveals at doors and windows. These strips also serve as strengtheners to prevent warping.

Windowsills are made by cutting special pieces a little wider than the rest to protrude through the window openings and form a narrow lip at the front.

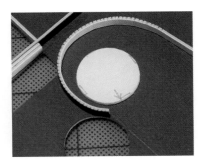

A strip is scored on the back to curve around the small circular window. The cutout circle of card is used to estimate the length required to form the reveal.

All the reveals and strengthening strips have been glued into position behind the rear wall.

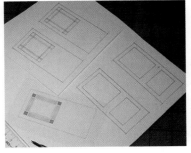

The four layers to form the door are traced on to thin card, and the coloured 'glass' panel is printed on to acetate with a desktop printer.

Interior openings are now cut away, and the edges painted a dark brown to avoid marking the acetate when painting edges after assembling.

All door layers have been glued together with the acetate in the middle. The outside edges have been trimmed, and a hole pierced for the doorknob.

A thin doorstop made from a narrow strip of card is glued inside the door opening, and a paper hinge has been glued to the door.

The paper hinge has been glued to the door frame and the door is tested for fit. A thin sliver has been trimmed from the bottom edge to prevent dragging.

All the windows have been traced on to thin card, and a little extra has been added around the outside of each, that can be glued to the back edges of the reveals.

The window frames have been cut from the card. It is not necessary to paint the edges, as the acetate can be glued to the back of the windows after painting.

The window frames have now been glued into place at the back of the reveals. (Note that the wall will not be glued to the rostrum until after painting.)

Strips of mount-board have been cut for the flat wooden trim and glued into position at the sides and top of the door and windows.

A strip of wooden dolls' house moulding has been cut with a saw and mitre box at 45° angles to fit neatly around the top piece of card.

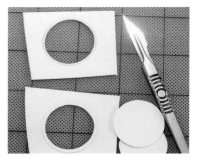

Construction of the decorative surround for the small round window begins by cutting carefully measured circles out of thin card.

The card circles have been glued together, trimmed, and cut into sections for the curved moulding. Pieces have been cut to form the wooden voussoirs.

All sections of the decorative surround for the circular window have now been assembled and glued into position.

The small return flat has been glued at the stage left end of the back run, and a skirting board made from layered card is applied at the bottom.

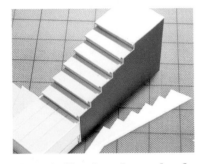

Thin card has been layered and cut to shape for the skirting board beside the main stairs, and the nosing has been trimmed away at each step for a good fit.

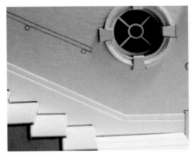

The sloping skirting board beside the main staircase has now been glued into position.

A second piece of shaped skirting board has been built and fitted in a similar manner, and glued to the flat beside the bottom steps of the staircase.

Pieces of thin card have been cut to be glued together in layers for the panelled facing at the on-stage side of the small landing.

The layered panel for the stair facing has been glued together, with a strip of mount-board added to top it off. It is now placed in position to check the fit.

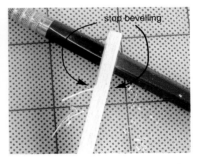

A piece of square-section obeché wood has been sawn to size for the newel post, and the edges carved with a scalpel to suggest 'stop-bevelling'.

163

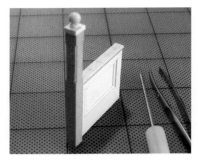

The newel post has been assembled with a small square and circle of card glued to the top and surmounted by a round-headed pin to simulate a finial.

Banisters are cut from 2mm-diameter dowel, and glued in position supporting a handrail made from strips of board glued together to the thickness required.

The hall area is now complete, and all the remaining flats for the main set have been traced on to mount-board from the working drawings, and cut out.

The three flats forming the section that juts towards the centre of the room have been assembled around mount-board formers to reinforce and hold the shape.

The section just constructed is placed temporarily in position against the main rostrum, and the large arch piece is tested for fit.

Strips of mount-board are glued into position for reveals around the inside of the arch, and extra strips are glued to the back to strengthen it and prevent warping.

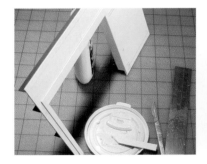

Mount-board strips have been cut and glued into place for the flat wooden arch surround. Reveals are covered with paper strips to hide the edges of the card layers.

The decorative fretwork piece for inside the arch has been traced on to card and the lengthy process of cutting out has begun, starting with the interior areas.

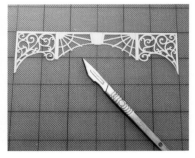

The fretwork has now been completely cut out. This piece required two and a half hours work, four scalpel blades, a large coffee and a small whisky.

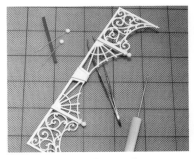

The two vertical upright pieces and the central 'keystone' shape have been cut from card and glued into place. Finials are made from pins and tiny pieces of card.

The built fretwork piece is now lightly fixed into position with tiny pinpoints of glue so that it can be removed later for easier painting.

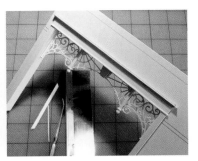

Dolls' house moulding has been glued to the top edge of the arch surround, and a thin strip of card is glued in place for the nosing at the bottom edge.

The long step at the downstage edge of the main rostrum is cut from mount-board, and supported and strengthened with strips cut to the correct width.

The step is glued to the main rostrum, and the arch flat is trimmed to fit, but not yet finally glued into position to allow it to be removed for later painting.

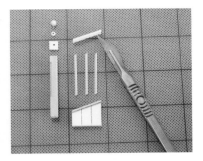

All the parts for the small handrail at the stage left end of the long step have been prepared, including stop-bevelling on the newel post.

The small handrail is completed and placed into position. It will not be finally glued in place until the model has been painted.

Strips of mount-board have been glued into position for the reveals to the opening in the down-stage right door flat, and extended to provide extra strength.

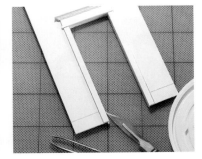

The door flat is turned over, and the flat door surround, moulding and nosing is added as before. Skirting board will be added at a later stage.

165

Panels have been cut from thin card to make the six-panelled door. This door is only seen from one side, so it is not necessary to panel the back.

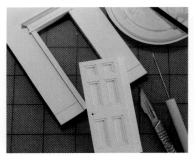

The layers of card for the door have been glued together, trimmed around the outside edges, and a strip of paper has been glued to the back for a hinge.

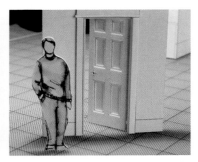

The paper hinge has been glued to the off-stage side of the reveal, and thin strips of card have been glued to the reveal for doorstops.

The flat immediately upstage of the door flat is strengthened by a gridwork of mount-board strips glued to the back.

The door flat is attached to the flat upstage of it, using mount-board brackets glued to the back to reinforce the join and maintain the correct angle.

Strips of cardboard skirting board are glued into place either side of the door. The next flat needs no skirting board, as it is hidden by kitchen furniture.

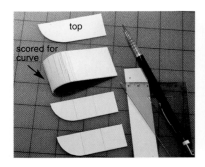

Parts for the kitchen counter have been cut from mount-board. The facing has been scored for the curved end. The top has been cut wider for the overhang.

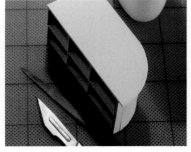

The assembled counter showing the inside supporting structure. The curved side of the top layer has been slightly rounded with a fine flat file.

Thin strips of card have been glued around the counter to suggest tongue and groove, and it has been placed in position with stools from the 3D printer.

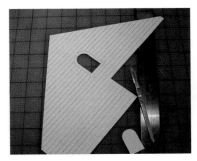

Attention now turns to the flown gable end. The drawing has been transferred to mount-board with graphite paper, and cut out.

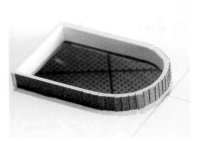

A strip of board has been glued to the back of the window opening to form a reveal. The round top section has been scored as usual for a smooth curve.

More strips of mount-board are glued to the back for extra strength. Fewer strips than usual are needed, as the front decoration will also add support.

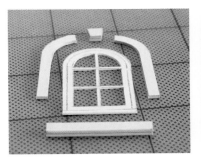

Pieces of card have been cut out to complete the small window. The sill and 'keystone' are built from two layered pieces of board for extra thickness.

The window is now complete, and paper strips have been glued inside the reveal to hide the edges of the card layers. Two under-sill supports will be added later.

Strips of thin card have been cut for the clapboard surface treatment, and these are now being glued into place slightly overlapping each other.

The cardboard strips are trimmed to fit neatly round the window, and the clapboard facing is now complete.

Outlines of the gable trims have been traced on to card, and the inside edges have been cut. The outside edges will be trimmed when they are glued together.

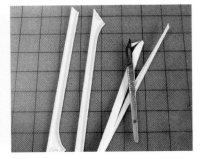

Cardboard layers for both gable trims have been glued together and trimmed around the outside edges.

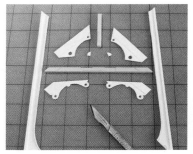

All pieces for the detailing on the gable end are cut out; the small circles have been removed with a leather punch, and stop-bevelling cut into the wood strips.

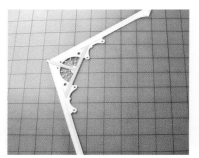

The decorative trim for the gable end has been assembled, and the detailing at the centre built from beads threaded on to wire and glued firmly into place.

The gable is now complete. Cardboard 'shingles' have been glued in place, and a coat of gesso has been applied to unify the various construction materials.

Crown mouldings built from wooden dolls' house coving and strips of mount-board are glued around the top edge of the main part of the set where required.

All crown mouldings, picture rails and skirting boards have now been glued in place.

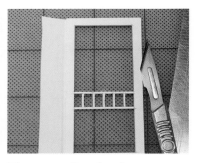

The screen door has been cut from card, and a paper hinge glued to the side. The screen mesh will be glued to the back of the door after painting.

The screen door's paper hinge has been glued to the back of the upstage door's reveal.

Parts for the porch behind the main door have been built from strips of obeché wood.

Sections of the porch are assembled and placed in position. The complete porch is not needed, as it will only be seen through the windows and door.

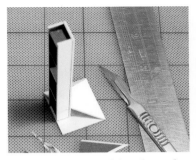

The extractor hood for above the cooker is under construction. The sloping parts near the bottom have been cut with carefully angled edges for a snug fit.

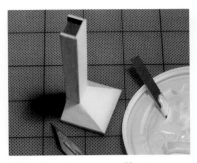

This piece is eventually to receive a smooth copper-like finish, so all surfaces are covered in firmly glued paper to hide the mount-board edges.

The moulding is cut away to allow the extractor chimney to pass through, and a model cooker pulled from recycled stock is tried for fit.

The model is now ready for painting, and all parts are tried in position with some of the furniture from the 3D printer and the ubiquitous scale figure.

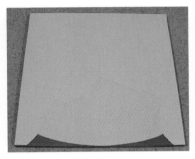

The plan has been traced on to mount-board, and cut to the shape of the forestage. The mount-board has then been glued to a sheet of heavy duty MDF.

Planked areas of the floor and rostrum have been based with raw umber, burnt umber, grey and Payne's grey using a hog-hair brush for a streaky texture.

Planks are defined and grained with coloured pencils, and the rostrum glued in place. Visible areas of the baseboard are painted black.

Walls of the main set have been based in a creamy grey gouache for the main part of the set, and green for the hall and stairs area.

The woodwork has now been painted and grained. Panelling and mouldings are emphasized using scene painters' techniques of shadows and highlights.

All the wood areas have been varnished, and coloured 'glass' fitted behind the round window. Black gauze has been glued into the screen door for mesh.

Nearly all the parts can now be glued into place on the baseboard. The stage-right wall is left separate until the kitchen units have been fitted.

The cooker hood has been painted with copper metallic paint, the top darkened with a little Payne's grey, and finally glued into position.

The flown gable is painted with a streaky mixture of mid-grey and raw umber. Parts beneath the trim have been darkened by working in some Payne's grey.

The clapboarding and gable trim have been further defined with highlights and shadows, and then glued together. The shingles have been painted dark brown.

Samples of the base colours have been kept during painting, and are now glued to a card for portable reference when shopping for set dressings.

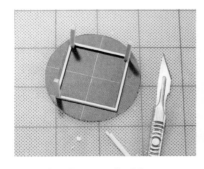

A top for the round table is cut from mount-board, and a square frame glued beneath. Legs are cut from wood and trimmed to fit neatly into each corner.

The circular table is now ready for painting, and is seen here with four dining chairs from the 3D printer.

A piece of foam board has been trimmed for the mattress of the cot-bed, and a piece of black-wrap from the electrical department has been cut for the cover.

The black-wrap bedcover has been painted dark red, then glued to the top of the foam board and 'draped' at the sides and corners.

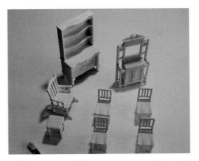

All pieces of furniture produced by the 3D printer have been painted with artists' gesso, using a small hog-hair brush to scrub the gesso into the plaster surface.

All the furniture pieces built so far have now been painted and sprayed with gloss fixative.

Kitchen units and the sink have been built from mount-board. It is not necessary to make doors practical here. Taps are dolls' house drawer knobs.

The kitchen units have been painted and given a shine with gloss picture varnish. Sink, taps and handles are painted with silver gouache.

Kitchen units and the stage-right wall are glued into position. Tiles are drawn on thin card with a 2H pencil, and glazed with picture varnish.

The fridge has been built from mount-board, and then painted with gouache and a coat of picture varnish. The handle is a small piece of 1.5mm dowel.

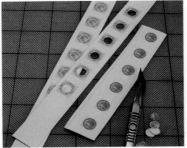

Plates downloaded from the Internet are printed to size on card, the centres cut out, and then glued together before final trimming to make a raised rim.

The trimmed plates are varnished to produce a gloss finish, and then glued in place on the kitchen dresser.

Carpets have been downloaded, adjusted in size and proportion as required, and printed on to card. White edges have been tinted with gouache.

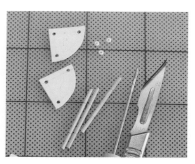

Parts have been cut from card, and 1.5mm dowel for the small 'what-not' to sit in the corner of the hallway, between the stairs and the door.

The corner 'what-not' glued together and painted with gouache, and a coat of picture varnish.

A structure built from strips of mount-board is glued to the back of the model to support the gable. On stage, the gable will be flown.

The 'flown' gable seen from the front of the model.

An armature for the small tree behind the upstage door is made from twisted electrical wire, and is now ready to be covered with tissue paper and paste.

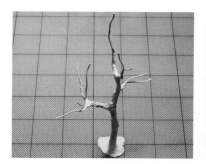

The tree, covered in tissue paper, paste and a coat of artists' gesso, is now ready to be painted.

One or two leaves cut from paper painted with gouache are glued to the tree. As the play takes place in autumn, only a few leaves are needed.

The set model is presented to the cast and the director at the first rehearsal of the play. The model box has just been removed for a clearer view.

BIBLIOGRAPHY

Bablet, D. *The Theatre of Edward Gordon Craig*
(Eyre Methuen, 1966)
Baldwin, P. *Toy Theatres of the World*
(A. Zwemmer Ltd., 1992)
Beard, G. *The Work of Christopher Wren*
(John Bartholomew and Son Ltd., 1982)
Carver, G. & White, C. *Computer Visualization for the Theatre:
3D Modelling for Designers* (Elsevier Ltd., 2003)
Dutton, M & Doran R. *Autodesk 3ds Max 8 Revealed*
(Thompson Course Technology, 2006)
Guégan, Y. & Le Puil, R. *The Handbook of Painted Decoration*
(W.W. Norton & Company Ltd., 1996)
Hofschröer, P. *Wellington's Smallest Victory –
The Duke, the Model Maker and the Secret of Waterloo*
(Faber and Faber Ltd., 2004)
Juracek, J. A. *Surfaces – Visual Research for Artists, Architects
& Designers* (W. W. Norton and Company, 1996)
Hoskins, L. *The Papered Wall – History, Pattern, Technique*
(Harry N. Abrams, Inc. New York, 1994)
McFarland, J. *Mastering Autodesk VIZ 2008*
(Wiley Publishing Inc. 2007)
McFarland, J. & Jinjer S. *Master VISUALLY 3ds Max 8*
(Wiley Publishing inc. 2006)
Meyer, F. S. *Handbook of Ornament*
(Dover Publications Inc., 1957)
Mills, C. *Designing with Models – A studio guide to making
and using architectural design models*
(John Wiley & Sons, 2005)
Morris, M. *Models: Architecture and the Miniature*
(John Wiley & Sons, 2006)
Orton, K. *Model Making for the Stage – A Practical Guide*
(The Crowood Press, 2004)
Payne, D. R. *Theory and Craft of the Scenographic Model*
(Southern Illinois University Press, 1985)
Ripley, D. *AutoCAD – A Handbook for Theatre Users*
(Entertainment Technology Press Ltd., 2005)
Roosendal, T. *et al. The Official Blender 2. 3 Guide – Free 3D
Creation Suite for Modeling, Animation, and Rendering*
(No Starch Press Inc., 2004)
Rosenfeld, S. *A Short History of Scene Design in Great Britain*
(Basil Blackwell, 1973)
Smith, A. C. *Architectural Model as Machine –
A New View of Models from Antiquity to the Present Day*
(Elsevier Ltd, 2004)
Smith, H. W. *The Art of Making Furniture in Miniature*
(Kalmbach Publishing Co, 1993)
Speaight, G. *The History of the English Toy Theatre*
(Studio Vista Ltd., 1969)
Speltz, A. *The Styles of Ornament*
(Dover Publications Inc., 1959)
Stewart-Wilson, M. *Queen Mary's Dolls' House*
(The Bodley Head Ltd., 1988)

Sykes, T. S. *AutoCAD 2008: One Step at a Time*
(Forager Publications, 2007)
Sykes, T. S. *3D AutoCAD 2008: One Step at a Time*
(Forager Publications, 2007)
Towner, M. *Dolls' House Furniture – The Collector's Guide
to Selecting and Enjoying Miniature Masterpieces*
(David & Charles, 2002)
Vincente, P. and Connor, T. *The Language of Doors*
(Artisan, a division of Workman Publishing Inc., 2005)
Winslow, C. *The Handbook of Set Design*
(The Crowood Press, 2006)
Winslow, C. *The Oberon Glossary of Theatrical Terms*
(Oberon Books Ltd., 1991)

WEB SITES

www.apple.com/quicktime/download – Download Quicktime, a free programme to display animations.
www.blender.org – Download Blender; a completely free, fully-fledged 3D modelling programme.
www.cs.ualberta.ca/~pierreb/VEDP1.htm – Dr Pierre Boulanger's site describing experiments in virtual reality at the University of Alberta and elsewhere.
www.cad4theatre.org.uk – David Ripley's site devoted to AutoCAD where you can sign up for his online course, or download the ABTT's recommended CAD standards.
www.dollshouseminiaturesofbath.com – Dolls House Miniatures of Bath is a supplier of quality dolls houses and furniture.
www.ema-models.co.uk – E.M.A. Model Supplies Ltd. UK based online suppliers of model making parts and materials.
www.WMRAonline.ca – The Edmonton Model Railway Association in Edmonton, Alberta, Canada.
www.equity.org.uk – Equity is a union representing actors, directors, designers and almost anyone professionally involved in theatre, television, films or performance of any kind. The Society of British Theatre Designers is affiliated with Equity.
www.modelshop.co.uk – The 4D Model Shop. London suppliers of a very wide range of equipment and materials for the model maker.
www.plastruct.com – Plastruct Inc. International suppliers of plastic materials and scale parts for model makers.
www.sketchup.com – Download a free version of Google SketchUp; a quick, user-friendly 3D modelling system.
www.theatredesign.org.uk – Society of British Theatre Designers. A professional organization for set, costume, lighting, video and sound designers.
www.vrtoolbox.com – Download a free demo of The VRWorx to create realistic interactive digital versions of set models.
www.winslow.uk.com – The author's personal web site.
www.zcorp.com – 3D printing systems by Z Corporation.

INDEX

3D printer 105, 106, 139, 140, 141, 142, 143
~ formats 140
3ds Max (3D Studio MAX) 129, 131, 132,
133, 140
ABTT (Association of British Theatre
Technicians) 132
access steps 42, 69
accountant 153
accuracy 57
acetate 44, 78, 79, 91, 108, 116
acrylic paint 92, 106, 124
actors 150, 151
Adams, Douglas 8
Additive Fabrication 139
adhesive 44
contact ~ 45
spray ~ 45, 55
~ tape 46
Adobe Photoshop 151
air, ~brush 94, 95, 100
~ supply 95
alginate 87
algorithms 131
aluminium 42
Appia, Adolph 15
arena 87
armature 123, 124, 125, 126, 127
art board 38
auditorium 72, 156
AutoCAD 100, 129, 130, 132, 133, 140,
143, 158
Autodesk 132, 133,
~ Viz 133
backcloth 73, 114, 115
backers 25
backlighting (backcloths) 116
Bakelite 43
balsa wood 40, 42, 60, 103, 108, 118
baluster 82, 86, 138
balustrade 82
bandage, plaster ~ 124
banister 60, 82, 83, 104
Baroque moulding 80
Bartered Bride, The 49
base 50, 72
bass wood 40, 42, 103
beads 63, 83, 109
bed cover 108
bit-map 129
black-wrap 44, 108
blades 31
Blender 134
blockboard 50, 72
blotting paper 39, 40, 108
Bohème, La 29
bookcase 109, 113
books, model ~ 23, 109
border (stage) 73, 108, 115
Bostik 45
box cutters 33
box, model ~ 56, 71, 72, 73
brass 42
etched ~ 41
soldering ~ 65
brick 88, 93, 97, 138
Bristol board 38

Bristol Old Vic 114
brocade effect 101
bronze 92
Brothers Grimm, The 23, 113
brush 92, 93
camel-hair ~ 92
hog-hair ~ 93
sable ~ 92
budget 25
butt join 58
CAD (Computer-Aided Design) 19, 129, 138
CAM (Computer-Aided Manufacturing)
138, 143
camera, digital ~ 129, 151
capital 84, 85, 86
capitals 81, 82
Captain Hook's sleigh 54
Caran d'Ache 92
card, corrugated ~ 73, 108
cutting ~ 57, 58
printer ~ 38
scoring ~ 18
ticket ~ 38
carpet 39, 40, 88
cartridge paper 39
Cast software 134
casting 84, 85, 86
cement, plastic ~ 45, 65
chair 104
arm~ 106
~rail 79, 91
rocking ~ 105
chandelier 119
Charley's Aunt 21
cheesecloth 127
Chinagraph pencil 108
circle stencil 38
circle, cutting ~ 61, 62
clogging 45
clutch pencil 37
CNC (Computer Numerical Control) 138
coat stand 158
colour 91
metallic ~ 92
~ range 92
~ samples 97
column 81, 82
barley-sugar ~ 82
fluted ~ 138
compasses 37, 95
compressor 95
concrete 143
contact adhesive 45
contour paste 80
copper 42
~ colour 92
soldering ~ 65
copyright 100, 152
corbel 86, 104
cord 127
Corel Photo-Paint 152
CorelDraw 100
Corinthian 81, 82
corner, mitred ~ 35, 58, 59
cornice 79
corrugated card 73

costume design 121, 122, 123
cotton, crochet ~ 94
~ sheeting 116
court, performances at ~ 11
Craft Mount 45
Craig, Edward Gordon 14, 15
crayon, wax ~ 91
Crimes of the Heart 20, 137, 144, 155, 156
157, 158
crochet cotton 94
Curious Labs 124, 135
curtains 106, 108
net ~ 108, 116
curve, cutting a ~ 61
fitting sides to a ~ 68
cushion 108
cut-cloth 115
cutters, side ~ 43
cutting, ~ card 57, 58
~ circles 61, 62
~ corners 58
~ curves 61
~ knife 31
~ mat 34
~ rule 32, 33
~ small parts 62
~ window panes 62
cyanoacrylate 43, 45, 47, 63, 78, 82, 106
111, 124, 142
cyc (cyclorama) 73, 150
DAS 84, 87
Davenant, Sir William 12
designer's colour 91
designs, transferring 40
digital, ~ camera 129, 151
~ skills 132
displaying the model 147
dividers, proportional ~ 56, 57
doll's house 7
~ furniture 104
~ people 123
door 75, 76
~ furniture 77, 104
hinging a ~ 76, 77
panelled ~ 76
Doric 81
dowel 118
cutting ~ 61
dpi (dots per inch) 129, 151
drafting 49
~ conventions 50
~ tape 46, 65
~ tools 36
drapes 73, 106, 107, 108
drawing 49
~ pins 118
dresser 110, 158
dressing 103, 108, 109
drinking straw 118
dye 116
electrical outlet 30, 148
elevation 53, 157
emery board 142
emulsion glaze 124
Equity (British Actors') 152, 153
etched brass 41

etching 138
experimental model 17
extrusion 131
fabric 44, 73, 106, 107, 121
fees 152
felt-tip pen 92
fence 109
fibreglass 127
field, raised ~ 77
figure, cutout ~ 122, 123
  digital ~ 124, 135
  human ~ 121, 148
file, needle ~ 35, 36
finial 104
fixatif 94
  applying ~ 95
fixative (see fixatif)
flag 108
flagstones 89, 98
flesh tone 124
flocked paper 39, 40, 88, 108
floor 87, 88
floorboard 88
flour and water paste 46
flown pieces 50, 72, 73, 113, 150
flux 46, 65, 66
flying system 113, 114
foam-core board 38, 59, 65, 72
foliage 126
forceps 35
Freeform Fabrication 139
fumes, noxious ~ 47
furniture 103, 104, 141, 142, 147, 152, 158
gauze 115, 116
gesso 42, 82, 83, 91, 106, 108, 124, 126, 127, 142
get-off 42, 69
glass, etching on ~ 138
glaze 97, 99
glazing bars, cutting out ~ 62, 63
Gloy 43
glue 43, 44, 64
gluing techniques 64
gold 92, 99
Google SketchUp 134
gouache 88, 91, 95, 97, 106, 108, 124, 142, 143
graphite 99, 143
  ~ paper 40, 55, 61, 80
grass 88
Great Model, The 8, 10
gypsum 143, 144
Habitat 103
hair, camel ~ 92
  hog ~ 93
  synthetic ~ 92, 93
handrail 42, 60, 82, 84, 85
hem-pocket 116
Henley, Beth 20, 155
highlight 96, 98
hinge 76
Hitchhiker's Guide to the Galaxy, The 8
Ikea 103
imperial system 55
IMSI/Design 134
inks, coloured ~ 78, 79, 89, 92, 95
interactive panoramic view 136
Ionic 81
iron 143
  painted ~ 99
ironwork, wrought ~ 75, 84
jewellery findings 109
join, butt ~ 59
  mitred ~ 59
Jones, Inigo 12

joystick 145
Kindersurprise eggs 109
knob 77, 105
ladder 42
lamp, practical ~ 119
  ~ bracket 63
laster cutter 138, 139
latex 85, 87
  ~ glaze 124
lathe 82
Latimer circle cutter 62
Layered Manufacturing 139
leather punch 35, 36
leaves 126
leg, stage ~ 73, 108
  furniture ~ 103
lift 119
light, ~ box 119
  ~ source 130, 131
lighting (a digital model) 131
  (a real model) 148
lighting 29, 96, 115, 119, 129
log-cabin 109
Loughborough University 143
Loutherbourg, Philip James de 13
luminaire 115, 131
magic 7, 8
manicure 142
marble 88, 97
mask, face 47
masking, stage ~ 72, 73, 108, 115
  ~ tape 46, 65
mat, cutting ~ 38
materials 38
Mathieu le Gros 94
matt board 38
MDF 50, 72
media, mixed ~ 91
megapixel 151
metal 42, 138
metal rule 32
Meyerhold, Vsevolod Emillevich 15
milling, ~ machine, digital ~ 143
Milliput 86
Ming Cho Lee 49
mink, Siberian 92
mitre box 34, 60, 79, 80
mitred corner 58
mixed media 91
model, ~ box 56, 71, 72, 73, 148
  computer-generated ~ 141
  conceptual ~ 17
  displaying a ~ 147
  exhibition of a ~ 25, 27
  experimental ~ 17
  digital ~ 24, 129, 130, 131, 134
  lighting a ~ 148
  photographing a ~ 151
  presentation of a ~ 22, 147, 148, 149
  sketch ~ 17
  virtual ~ 137
  white-card ~ 20, 147
modelling 84
mould 85, 87
  silicone ~ 86
moulding 60, 104
  Baroque ~ 80
  cardboard ~ 79
  dolls' house ~ 79
  Rococo ~ 80
mount-board 60, 61, 104, 108, 115, 117, 126
moving parts 113
museum board 38
muslin 127

nail varnish remover 47
needle, ~ file 35, 36
  sewing ~ 122, 123
newel post 82
NIC (National Insurance Contributions) 152, 153
non-slip rule 33
nosing 67
Nuova, Opera ~ 22, 23, 75, 113, 129, 142, 149
nurbs 131
obeché wood 40, 88, 103
octent 140
OISTAT 25
Opera Nuova 22, 23, 75, 113, 129, 142, 149
orders, classical ~ 81
organic features 84, 121, 127
organza 78, 115
Orton, Joe 19
painting 91
paintings 111
palette knife 93
panel, recessed ~ 76
panelling 79
panoramic view 136
Paperchase 108
papier maché 46, 80, 108, 124
parquet 39, 88, 91
paste 43, 123
  contour ~ 80
  flour and water ~ 46
  modelling ~ 124
paterae 36
pea bulb 119
pen, ruling ~ 95, 96
pencil 36, 55
  aquarelle ~ 98
  clutch ~ 37
  Chinagraph ~ 108
  coloured ~ 91, 92
  watercolour ~ 92, 97, 98
people 121, 123, 124
Périchole, La 22
Peter Pan 50, 51, 52, 53, 54, 127
pewter 92
Phantom of the Opera, The 119
photographing the model 151
Photoshop 152
picture rail 79, 91
pilaster 82, 86
pillar 80, 81, 82, 83
pillow 108
Pitlochry Festival Theatre 39, 85
pixel 129
plan, stage ~ 51, 155
plank 91
plaster 80, 87, 93
  ~ bandage 124
  dental ~ 85, 86
  ~ of Paris 93
plastic, ~ rods 42
  ~ sheet 58
Plasticine 65, 85, 87, 107, 108
Plastiweld 45
Plastruct 41
Plastruct 45
plates 109, 110, 111, 158
platform 51, 67, 116, 117
pliers 43
  angle-nose ~ 44, 106
plotter 142
plywood 50, 72
Pollock, Benjamin 9
Polyfilla 93, 126, 127
polystyrene 38, 39, 65, 127, 143

polyvinyl acetate (*see* PVA)
portfolio   151
Poser   124, 135
poster colour   92
poster paper   39
Prague Quadrennial Exhibition   25, 26
presentation   147, 148, 150
primitives   130
printer, ~ card   38
   ~/plotter   142
probe, biological ~   35
production meeting   20, 50, 147, 150
proportional dividers   56, 57
props   108, 109, 135
proscenium   50, 71, 72, 148, 156
punch, leather ~   35, 36
PVA   44, 45, 64, 66, 93, 116, 123
Queen Mary's dolls' house   107
Queen Victoria   93
QuickTime   136, 137
railing   84, 85
railway, model ~   8, 127
Rapid Prototyping   139
ray-tracing   131
Red Deer College   148
rendering   131
respirator   47, 95
Revell   45
revolving stage   117, 118
Ribbon   123, 143
rice paste   46
risers   69, 71
rocks   127
Rococo moulding   80
roller (backcloth)   114, 115
Rookery Nook   39
rostra (*see* rostrum)
rostrum   51, 67, 68, 119, 150, 151
rotation   131
rug   88
ruler, scale ~   37, 55, 56
ruling pen   95, 96
sable, Kolinsky ~   93
safety precautions   46
saw   34, 60, 80
SBTD (Society of British Theatre Designers)   25, 153
scale   103, 121
   working to ~   55, 56
   changing ~   56
Scale Link   41
scalpel   32
scanner   152
scene change   72, 73, 113
scene painting   96, 100
schools tour   113, 149
scissors   32
scrim   115, 116
section   53, 157
Seige of Rhodes, The   12
Sellotape   46
Serlio, Sebastiano   13
set square   37
setting up a model for presentation   147
shadow   96
Shakespeare, William   7, 11
sharkstooth   116
Siborne, Captain William   10, 11
side cutters   43
sightlines   51
silicone moulding paste   87
silver   92, 99
site-specific   147
size, glue ~   43
skirting board   79, 91

skull   86
smoke   138
software packages   132
soldering, ~ equipment   46
   ~ gun   46
   ~ iron   46, 47, 65, 66
   ~ techniques   65
solid modelling   130
Spectrum Z510 (3D printer)   139, 141, 143, 158
spindle   105
spline   130
spotlight (miniature)   119
spray adhesive   45, 47, 55, 108, 115, 118
St. Matthew Passion   14
St. Paul's Cathedral   8, 10
stage plan   51, 155
stained glass   78
stairs   42, 69, 71
   curved ~   70
Stanley   32, 33
stencil   100, 101
stencil, ~ circle   38
steps   69, 71
   access ~   42, 69
stereoscopic vizor   145
sticky tape   46
STL (Standard Tesselation language)   140
stonework   88, 89, 97
storage space   30
stove, pot-bellied ~   143
strawboard   34
Street Scene   29, 75, 129
strengthening techniques   66
string   126, 127
stringer   53, 69, 71
stucco   93, 97
studio, setting up a ~   29
superglue   43, 45, 47, 63, 78, 106, 142
surfaces, metallic ~   99
   painted ~   96, 98, 99
Swann-Morton   33
synthetic resin glue   45, 64, 65
syringe   64, 80
tablecloth   108
tactical model making   25
Tales of Hoffman, The   142
tape, ahesive ~   46
   drafting ~   46, 65, 147
   mounting ~   46
   sticky ~   46
tax, paying ~   152
technical drawing   49, 157
texture, painted ~   98, 147
texturing   91
Theatr Clwyd   50, 51, 52, 53, 54, 127, 130
theatre in-the-round   87, 147
Theatre Royal, York   21
thread   94, 123
ticket card   38
tile-work   91, 97
Timms Centre for the Arts   24, 137, 155, 156
tinning   66
tissue paper   40, 123, 126, 127
tomb, Egyptian ~   7
tools   31
   drafting ~   36
toothbrush   89
toxic fumes   138
toy theatre   7, 9
track   117
transferring designs   40
transparency   116
trap doors   50, 119
treads   69, 71

open ~   41, 69
Treasure Island   130
tree   121, 124, 125, 126, 127
tripod   151
trompe l'oeil   96, 97, 98
Trotec Speedy 300 laser cutter   138
truck   49, 116, 117
tumbler (backcloth)   114, 115
TurboCAD   134
turf   88
turntable   117, 118, 134
tweezers   35, 106
Twelfth Night   85
Uhu   43, 44, 64, 66
undercut   85, 86, 87
University of Alberta   144
upholstery tacks   118
varnish   88, 94, 97, 98, 99, 103, 104, 142
Vaseline   87, 108
vector graphics   129
veneer   42
Victoria and Albert Museum   103
Village of Idiots   122
virtual reality   144
Viz (3D Studio Viz)   133
   ~ Room   144
vizor, stereoscopic ~   145
VRML (Virtual Reality Modelling Language)   140
VRWorx   136, 137
wagon   116
wallpaper   99, 100, 101
   brocade ~   101
warp   66, 118
waste bin   30, 32
watercolour   88, 89, 91, 95
   ~ pencils   92, 97
Waterloo, Battle of   10, 11
wax crayon   91, 92
Webb, John   12
Weill, Kurt   129
Wellington, Duke of   10
What the Butler Saw   17, 19, 24, 103
wheels   117
white glue   44
winch   118
window   77, 91
   stained glass ~   78
   ~ types   78
window panes, cutting out ~   62, 63
Winsor and Newton   93
wire   43, 83, 85, 123, 124, 125
   ~ frame   130
   ~ mesh   127
   ~ snippers   43
Wolf Trap   121, 122
wood   40, 42
   balsa ~   40, 42, 60, 103, 108, 118
   bass ~   40, 42, 103
   cutting ~   60
   obeché ~   40, 88, 103
   painted ~   97
   ply~   50, 72
   polished ~   93
working drawing   53, 125, 156, 158
workspace   29
World Wide Web   152
Wren, Sir Christopher   8, 10
wrought ironwork   75, 84
WYSIWYG   134
X-Acto   32, 33, 34
XYZ octent   140
Z Corporation   139